Sincerely, Scott Neumann

Sincerely, Scott Neumann

Lane Strauss

Writers Club Press
San Jose New York Lincoln Shanghai

Sincerely, Scott Neumann

Published by Writers Club Press
an imprint of iUniverse.com, Inc.

For information address:
iUniverse.com, Inc.
620 North 48th Street
Suite 201
Lincoln, NE 68504-3467
www.iuniverse.com

ISBN: 0-595-12557-3

Printed in the United States of America

This book is dedicated to the guy who invented stupidity.

FOREWORD

My husband is a loser. I apologize.

—Cathy Strauss

PREFACE

I typed some e-mail. I sent it. Somebody responded. This continued over several months. I kept the good ones. I threw out the bad ones. What else do you need to know?

ACKNOWLEDGEMENTS

I want to thank Steve for his countless hours of help and useless formatting. My next door neighbor Brent for letting me use his name and all of his tools. And family and friends who have done absolutely nothing to support me along the way.

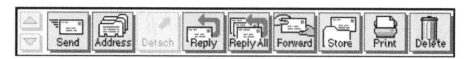

From: scott47@yipee.com
Sent: Wednesday, 3 June
To: Framing Gallery (ninth@blahblahblah.com)
Subject: framing query

Dear Picture Framing People:

Last week, on my 33rd birthday, my parents surprised me by giving me the excess flesh that was cut off my penis when I was circumcised as a baby. I had no idea people were allowed to keep "the lost skin", let alone that my parents still had mine!

Anyway, they've been keeping it in liquid in a canning jar to preserve the color and texture, but now that I have it, I'm thinking about a shadow box or something more appealing to the eye than a simple glass jar.

When people look at it above our fireplace, I want them to think, "Wow, what a beautifully designed piece," as opposed to, "Hey, isn't that dead penis skin?"

Any help you can suggest with this would be greatly appreciated.

Sincerely,

Scott Neumann

aka, Muhammad Abdul Lazman Hazeh

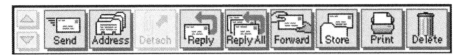

From: darin <ninthst@blahblahblah.com
Sent: Wednesday, 3 June
To: scott47@yipee.com
Subject: picture frame

Mr. Neumann,

Thank you for visiting our website. As for your inquiry into shadow box frames, or the framing of objects, we do specialize in this sort of custom framing. While we have had vast experience in framing several rather interesting objects, I must admit that request is rather unique. I think it would be quite a rewarding challenge, we would love to assist you in this delicate matter.

If you should have any questions please feel free to email or call.

Thank you,
Michael

From: scott47@yipee.com
Sent: Thursday, 6 August
To: Restaurant Manager(bill@blahblahblah.com)
Subject: complaint

Dear Food Service People:

I have a complaint about your restaurant. The food is excellent, but your floor isn't level. Ever since I ate there last week, my equilibrium has been thrown off. Yesterday I walked into two walls, and the other day I nearly stepped into an open elevator shaft. I have also been unable to ride my son's tricycle.

The reason I know it's your floor is because I lived in an apartment once where the hardwoods were off by 3 degrees. I had severe bruises all over my body from walking into tables, lamps and my roommate. Your restaurant was the only variation in my routine during the course of last week, so it has to be you.

I'm sure I'm not the first person to complain about this. I can't even imagine what would happen if someone walked in with vertigo.

Sincerely,

Scott Neumann
AAAAAAAAAAAAAAAAAAAAAAAAAAAAAAAAAAAAAAAAAAAA Painters

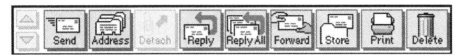

From: Bill <bill@blahblahblah.com>
Sent: Friday, 7 August
To: scott47@yipee.com
Subject: complaint

Good Afternoon Scott—

I was sorry to read about the problems you have experienced since your recent visit to our restaurant. If you could provide me with a little more information-which location you were visiting, which area of the restaurant you noticed the problem, time of day, etc.—I will be able to investigate your comments in greater detail. I did forward your message to our construction/maintenance department and we are waiting for your response.

Bill
Restaurant Manager

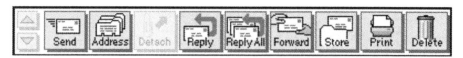

From: scott47@yipee.com
Sent: Tuesday, 23 June
To: Pastor (stluke@blahblahblah.com)
Subject: personal crisis

Dear Pastor Person Sir:

I've recently gone through some intense personal drama in my life and I'm not quite sure how to deal with it.

Last weekend while driving to visit my parents, I came upon a swampy area near their home. Sir, the humidity was thick and unbearable, and as I kept driving, I came to a horrible realization: thousands of bugs were smashing on my windshield! I attempted to avoid these poor innocent creations of God, but it was impossible. They were everywhere. SPLAT! The sound was horrific. By the time I arrived at my parent's home, I could barely speak. We joined hands in our nightly family prayer and I went off to bed.

Pastor, I can't begin to tell you the feelings of sorrow I had the next morning. The entire front of our car was covered with this "bug genocide". Understand that I have never killed a living thing in my life, and now not only have I murdered thousands, but I'm forced to scrape their dead bodies off of my headlights! My wife has attempted to console me through our faith and belief in the Lord Jesus Christ, but I can never, ever erase the sight of those lost, unwitting creatures being pounded to mutilated, tortured twisted death because of my lead foot.

I am at a loss. As are thousands of bug families. Help.

Sincerely,
Scott Neumann

P.S. Do you sell hats or t-shirts with the logo of your church?

From: stluke@blahblahblah.com
Sent: Tuesday, 23 June
To: scott47@yipee.com
Subject: question

Dear Scott:

I received your E-mail and I was a little confused as to why you would be that upset over such an occurrence. Let me assure you that it is not recorded in Scripture that any of God's creations except for humans have eternal souls.

Therefore, please be assured that those bugs were put here simply as a food source for some of God's other creatures and in no way should you condemn yourself for such an innocent act. I know the God that we know and serve would not hold us accountable for such an inadvertent act. I hope that helps.

In response to your question, no, I'm sorry, we have no T-shirts or caps.

Sincerely,

E. Jennings, Pastor

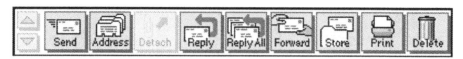

From: scott47@yipee.com
Sent: Wednesday, 27 May
To: Smoke Shop (ber1@blahblahblah.com)
Subject: new product

Dear Tobacco-Selling People:

By using applied technologies and conclave diametric compounds, I have developed a cigarette that gets longer when you smoke it.

I believe my cigarette will revolutionize the tobacco industry. The name of my cigarette brand is "Longers." Our advertising theme is: "Longers. 18¾ inches of full tobacco pleasure." They have an oniony/charcoal flavor and are plaid in color.

Would you have any interest in carrying Longers on a limited basis? If so, I can ship some to you immediately. Please let me know ASAP. I've got root canal surgery in 45 minutes.

Sincerely,

Scott Neumann,

President and CEO, Longers Brand Cigarettes. Ex-president and CEO, Widers Brand Cigarettes—"The Cigarette That Barely Fits In Your Mouth"

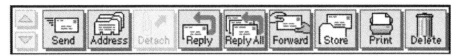

From: Ber1@blahblahblah.com
Sent: Wednesday, 27 May
To: scott47@yipee.com
Subject: new product

GOT YOUR E-MAIL ABOUT YOUR CIGARETTE'S, ARE YOU SENDING OUT SAMPLES??????? A PRODUCT LIKE THIS IS BETTER IF I COULD LET THEM SEE A SAMPLE

LET US KNOW

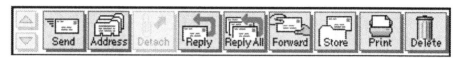

From: scott47@yipee.com
Sent: Thursday, 6 August
To: FM Radio Station (majic@blahblahblah.com)
Subject: song request

Dear Radio Station Request Line People:

I've been listening to your station for a while now and I'm wondering why you never play "If You Could Read My Mind, Love", by Gordon Lightfoot. This is my favorite song.

I like the words of "If You Could Read My Mind, Love", by Gordon Lightfoot. I like Gordon Lightfoot's voice. And I think the tune of "If You Could Read My Mind, Love" is extremely catchy.

I realize "If You Could Read My Mind, Love", by Gordon Lightfoot is not a new song, but it's a good song. And I think if you played "If You Could Read My Mind, Love", by Gordon Lightfoot, people will remember what a nice song it is. It being, "If You Could Read My Mind, Love", by Gordon Lightfoot.

I also like "The Edmund Fitzgerald", by Gordon Lightfoot, but not as much as "If You Could Read My Mind, Love", by Gordon Lightfoot.

If I could ever get through to make a request, I would request "If You Could Read My Mind, Love", by Gordon Lightfoot. I hope to hear back from you soon. I also hope to hear "If You Could Read My Mind, Love", by Gordon Lightfoot soon, too.

Sincerely,

Scott Neumann,

Aero-Tastylick Food Corp.

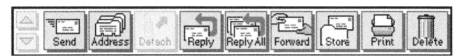

From: Station Mail<majic@blahblahblah.com
Sent: Thursday, 6 August
To: scott47@yipee.com
Subject: song request

Scott,

Our format is Urban Adult Contemporary, so the majority of the music
we play is by African-American artists. While I am personally a fan of Mr.
Lightfoot's tunes, I think most of our audience would likely find them
somewhat out of place. For the same reason, we don't usually air rock,
country, classical and many other genres.

Thanks for your inquiry.

Jon S.
Website Content Manager

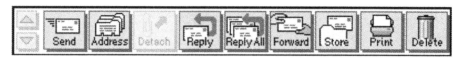

From: scott47@yipee.com
Sent: Sunday, 23 August
To: Citrus Juice Company (PRINCE@blahblahblah.com)
Subject: product information request

Dear Orange Juice-Making People:

I don't really like the taste of your orange juice, but the container it comes in is delicious!!! The texture is superb, and combined with the tart flavor of an orange, well, you clearly have a confectionery delight! Can you refer me to your container-manufacturing partner? I'd really like to get in contact with them and find out how I can order a supply of their paper products on my own.

I hope I haven't offended you. I'm sure that even an outstanding company such as yours receives some negative feedback from time to time. But I also wanted to congratulate you. Your oranges soaked nicely into the packaging. Great job!

Sincerely,

Dr. Scott Neumann, Chief of Staff, Neumann Urgi-Nosebleed Centers, Inc.

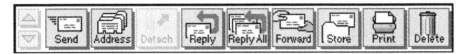

From: PRINCE@blahblahblah.com
Sent: Tuesday, 25 August
To: scott47@yipee.com
Subject: customer relations

Dear Mr. Neumann:

Thank you for taking the time to write to us at our Web Site. We appreciate the time you took to share your comments with us.

Thanks so much for the compliment. The carton manufacturer can be found on the side panel under the folded triangular closure. If you have any further questions or need more help, please feel free to contact us again.

Thanks again for writing! As our Customer, you are very important to us. We value your comments, and will look forward to all future opportunities to serve you. Thank you for shopping with us.

Sincerely,

Bobbi P.
Customer Relations

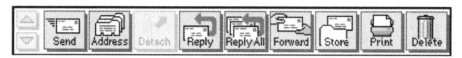

From: scott47@yipee.com
Sent: Thursday, 25 June
To: Talent Agent (mitch@blahblahblah.com)
Subject: model applicant

Dear Modeling Agency People:

I would like to apply for a position with your agency as a knuckle model. I am 5'11, 185, medium build, black/gray hair and greenish eyes. Basically, I'm average. However, I've have been told on more than one occasion that I possess a perfect set of knuckles. How do I go about creating a knuckle portfolio? Are their photographers that specialize in male hands? Are they gay? I'm bi-curious. Any advice you can provide me with would be appreciated.

I just don't want to look back at my life, staring at these magnificent bumps on my hands, wondering what I could have been.

Sincerely,

Scott Neumann, CPA, MD, RN, BLT

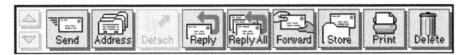

From: mitch <mitch@blahblahblah.com
Sent: Monday, 29 June
To: scott47@yipee.com
Subject: model applicant

HI SCOTT,

I REPRESENT two people at the moment for hand modeling. I would love to shoot your comp cards, showing your knuckles and all the looks they can achieve. What do you think?

MITCH

From: scott47@yipee.com
Sent: Monday, 29 June
To: Detective Agency (info@blahblahblah.com)
Subject: detective assistance

Dear Spying On Other People People:

I live in a suburb of Cleveland, and I have reason to believe that some-one is stealing my front lawn.

Over the last few months, I've noticed suspicious areas of brown which have appeared in my yard. I've come to the conclusion that at some point during the day or night, small patches of grass are being taken off my lawn, roots and all. I'm almost positive that it's my neighbor, Brent Fiorucci. He always makes comments about how nice my lawn looks and how crappy his does. All of a sudden, he's not saying anything. And his lawn looks great—like mine used to.

I would like your assistance in keeping a 24-hour watch on my front yard for 3 days. I really want to nail this fucker. How much would you charge for something like this?

Obviously I would give you the key to my house so you could use the crapper. The fridge is fair game, too. But you're on your own with beer.

Sincerely,

Scott Neumann,
Associate Director, Veterinary Medicine Hospital for Aged Felines.

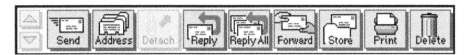

From: Jan<info@blahblahblah.com
Sent: Monday, 29 June
To: scott47@yipee.com
Subject: detective assistance

Hi Scott,

I am in Connecticut, unless you want to pay to fly me there, pay all hotel and meal expenses, plus surveillance, I think it would be a lot cheaper to get someone close by.

Good Luck, Jan

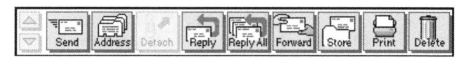

From: scott47@yipee.com
Sent: Tuesday, 17 February
To: Baseball Equipment Manufacturers (gs@blahblahblah.com)
Subject: Product inquiry

Dear Sports Training Equipment People:

I have a question about your Double Wheel Pitching Machine.

My eight-year-old son Brent Fiorucci Neumann plays little league. He's a good second baseman—damned good-—mainly because I've trained him by hitting line drives from the pitcher's mound and not letting him use a glove.

Anyway, I think he needs some work with his hitting. He only hit .667 last year. My question is this: How long does it take your machine to reach 100 miles an hour? I don't mean in time, I'm talking about distance. I mean, if the machine was 10 feet from home plate, what speed would the ball be when it got there? And could I make it faster?

If I can change his reaction time to hit a ball close and fast, they may never get him out.

I look forward to hearing back from you. I've heard that you're one tough company. I'm a tough SOB, too.

Sincerely,

Rev. Scott Neumann

P.S. Can I aim the machine to pitch high and inside?

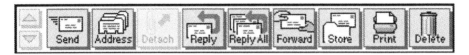

From: gs@blahblahblah.com
Sent: Wednesday, 18 February
To: scott47@yipee.com
Subject: baseball equipment

Dear Rev. Neumann:

Thank you for visiting our website and your interest in our products.

Regarding your e-mail, we do not have a calculation for any of our Machine's being placed at 10 feet from home plate. We strongly caution and do not recommend using any of our machines less than 30 feet from home plate. Due to the high potential injury factor of a pitching machine at this close distance, we can not advise or assist a customer using the equipment in this manner.

Thank you for your e-mail message.

From: scott47@yipee.com
Sent: Wednesday, 28 January
To: Petroleum Company (AL@blahblahblah.com)
Subject: service

Dear Service Station People:

I wanted to let you know that you have some really terrific people running your gas stations.

I recently filled my car at the station near my house. My total was $12.01. When I got inside, I realized that I had forgotten my wallet. The attendant told me not to worry about it, because his friends came and got gas all the time and he never makes them pay, either. He even gave me some of his marijuana. Good stuff! I could barely drive home. I think his name was Doug. Do you have some type of company award that goes to employees who go above and beyond the call of duty? I think he deserves it.

Thank you for your time.

Sincerely,

Scott Neumann

Honorary Citizen of The Day, October 23rd, 1983

From: AL@blahblahblah.com
Sent: Wednesday, 28 January
To: scott47@yipee.com
Subject: service

Dear Mr. Neumann:

Thank you for your recent Internet communication. Comments from our customers help us to do a better job. We consider customer service a top priority at our company. It is important for you to know that all retail outlets are independently operated and that the parent company does not control our independent dealers' operating practices. We would be happy to investigate this situation and get the dealer's reason for his policy if you can let us know what station you are referring to (name of the business, address or city). You mentioned that the employee's name was Doug. Can you also let us know what day and time you were in the station? You can send us this information via e-mail again. Thank you for bringing this matter to our attention and giving us the opportunity to respond.

Sincerely,
Amy L.
Customer Relations
Credit Card Center

From: scott47@yipee.com
Sent: Thursday, 17 September
To: Cemetery/Memorial Home (BeforeNee@blahblahblah.com)
Subject: job applicant

Dear Helper Of Dead People Person:

I am currently searching for a position as a funeral home spiritual director.

Sirs, for two decades in my role as "Elgin, the Clown from Heaven", I have delighted grieving friends and families by helping them realize that a funeral doesn't have to be such a somber event.

My act lasts for about 20 minutes, and some of my songs include "Isn't That St. Peter?", "Wow, It Really Is A Big White Light", and the old favorite, "Pine? I'm Not Good Enough For Oak?"

On occasion (i.e., the Iowa school bus crash of 1978), I have performed for 5 or 6 families in a day. One woman even asked to sit through another funeral because "she was going to a movie to not think about the fact that her husband was run over by a gasoline truck, but I was better."

I would welcome the opportunity to meet with you soon, and discuss any opportunities you may be aware of in your area. I think you'll find that I could bring a lot to the party. And when I say party, I mean it!

Sincerely,
Scott Neumann

Hoping To Make Every Funeral More Of A FUN-eral.

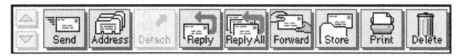

From: BeforeNee@blahblahblah.com
Sent: Friday, 18 September
To: scott47@yipee.com
Subject: job applicant

Thank you for your interest in Mount Sinai Memorial Park. At this time there is no opening suitable for your talents. Good luck in your search.

W. White
Sales Manager

From: scott47@yipee.com
Sent: Wednesday, 21 October
To: Famous Quotations (j@blahblahblah.com)
Subject: quote

Dear "Who Said That?" People:

I am having a hard time finding the source for a famous quote which is one of my favorite things to say: "Dammit Mother, you smell like burning cheesecloth again!"

Any help you could provide me would be greatly appreciated. I hope to hear back from you soon.

Sincerely,
Scott Neumann

1998 Co-Champion, Milwaukee Barefisted Boxing Championships.

From: j@blahblahblah.com
Sent: Thursday, 22 October
To: scott47@yipee.com
Subject: famous quotations

We regret that this is a quote we are unfamiliar with. Our database search offers no matches for the word "cheesecloth." You might try one of the quotation databases on the Web:

http://www.lexmark.com/data
http://www.columbia.edu/acis/bartleby/bartlett
http://www.nhmccd.cc.tx.us/lrc/kc/quotation-subject.html

J. Johnson
Computing Support Services

From: scott47@yipee.com
Sent: Monday, 22 June
To: Interior Designers (decor@blahblahblah.com)
Subject: complaint

Dear Carpeting People:

I just had my home carpeted with some royal blue Berber carpeting from one of your competitors. And I'm royally pissed.

We have two bedrooms in our home which are exactly the same size. Yesterday, I counted 142,768 carpeting loops in my son's bedroom, and only 141,882 in my daughter's. I'm wondering why this happened. Did our carpeting come from two different lots? The installers did seem to be giggling a lot as they were putting the carpeting down. I thought they were gay, but now I'm not so sure. Are we being shortchanged in any way with a "larger loop"?

Sirs, I typically don't resort to challenging people I do business with, but wouldn't you agree that seems to be a significant difference? To me, an 884 variance in loops seems like a lot.

I've heard good things about you and I'm now regretting I went with these scam artists.

Sincerely,
Scott Neumann

P.S. Just to be sure I don't make an ass out myself, I'm having my wife count them one more time.

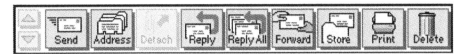

From: decor@blahblahblah.com
Sent: Tuesday, 23 June
To: scott47@yipee.com
Subject: carpeting

Scott,

Reminds me of a song from the 80's to much time on my hands. I can't
believe you counted the loops! But to answer your question: It can be that
the carpet in one room was stretched and trimmed tighter than the other.
I was wondering is there really a big difference in the two rooms such as
space between the loops to cause you to count them. Also it could be that
the carpet was irregular.
I don't know where you bought it but some places sell irregular carpets.
Well I hope this helps let me know.

Mister Decor

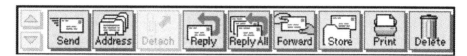

From: scott47@yipee.com
Sent: Wednesday, June 3
To: Card company (hdavis@blahblahblah.com)
Subject: new card line

Dear Cards For All Occasion People:

I have recently written and designed a full line of greeting cards for obese people. My card line is called "Huskies."

Sirs, to someone who has never been large, it is often difficult to explain the special bond that exists between big, fat, overweight people and other big, fat overweight people. Huskies let them know that there's someone special who understands their place in the world. Their big, fat overweight place.

Here is a representative sample from my line:

FRONT: I HATE WHEN I HEAR THAT FAT PEOPLE ARE LAZY, STUPID AND POSSESS NO SELF-CONTROL.

INSIDE: I'M NOT STUPID.

As you can see, with the Huskies, I'm really hoping to reach that emotional level of understanding that bigger people can relate to. I currently have 150 cards in my collection, which I'm hoping to have in stores by the end of the year. If you have any interest in carrying Husky Cards, please respond via e-mail and I will get back to you ASAP. Initial response on the line has been good. The edible birthday card has been a big hit!

Sincerely, Scott Neumann

P.S. I'm sure you're wondering. 5'3", 316 lbs.

From: hdavis@blahblahblah.com
Sent: Monday, 8 June
To: scott47@yipee.com
Subject: greeting cards

Scott:

Your email message suggests that you may already have a line of cards printed. Gibson does not usually consider licensing a card line unless it has already achieved success in the marketplace. We would be more likely to consider purchasing one or more pieces of editorial.

We look forward to hearing from you.

H. Davis
Writing Manager

From: scott47@yipee.com
Sent: Friday, 19 June
To: Resort (snun@blahblahblah.com)
Subject: bed and breakfast

Dear Bed and Breakfast People:

I am looking for a quiet weekend getaway for my wife and I as we celebrate our tenth anniversary in November.

The reason I'm writing so far in advance is that my wife has allergies, and I want to make sure that wherever we go, she will not be exposed to anything that could precipitate one of her allergic reaction.

This is what Maryanne is allergic to: dust, tinfoil, plastic, blue chalk, paper, rocks, scissors, old batteries, the smell of electricity, anything red, crayons, unleaded gasoline, balsa wood, I Can't Believe It's Not Butter, french poodles, Cup Of Noodles, anyone who doodles, spray starch and 3-way bulbs.

If you could get back to me if any of these pose a problem, that would be appreciated. However, if everything is OK, I would like to book a reservation for the weekend of November 12.

Sincerely,

Scott Neumann

Barber Pole Stripe Painter

From: snunn@blahblahblah.com
Sent: Thursday, 25 June
To: scott47@yipee.com
Subject: bed and breakfast

Hi and thanks for contacting us about our lovely inn on the gulf. I'm afraid after reading your e-mail that I can only say I'm so sorry for your wife, Maryanne. It must be terrible to be allergic to so many everyday items.

Unfortunately, there are several items on her list of allergens that she could not escape from here or really anywhere else for that matter, we of-course have electricity and although our rooms are immaculate, I'm sure there are dust particles in the air in general. Although I must admit not understanding how anyone could be allergic to 3 way bulbs and not regular bulbs, we have both!

Again, I appreciate you contacting us, but I'm afraid anything here could possibly make her ill. Normally I would refer you to another property or another company but honestly can't think of anyone anywhere who could assure her of no allergens such as the ones listed. I wish I could be more helpful. She couldn't escape some of these even in a hospital.

Sincerely,
Sue Nunn
Innkeeper
Park Inn

From: scott47@yipee.com
Sent: Wednesday, 11 February
To: Pastor (fcf@blahblahblah.net)
Subject: conversion issue

Dear Religious Leader-Type Person:

I am a recent convert to Catholicism after 36 years as a practicing Jew. I find the beliefs and mores of the Catholic faith to be more in line with my views and feelings that those of Judaism. However, as part of my conversion, my priest is recommending that I allow him to perform a "reverse circumcision" to separate myself from the Jewish faith.

While this seems a bit extreme to me, I am leaning towards doing it because I have a great deal of respect for my priest. Also, his brother manages my stock portfolio. Have you ever done one of these? My wife isn't too happy about this, by the way. She likes Mr. Whistle just the way he is.

I would appreciate any advice you have to offer.

Sincerely,
Scott Neumann

P.S. When you hear "Neumann" do you automatically think "Jew"? Maybe I should change my last name.

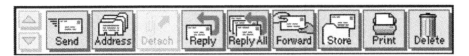

From: fcf@blahblahblah.net
Sent: Thursday, 12 February
To: scott47@yipee.com
Subject: conversion

Dear Scott,

I can see how you may be concerned about this situation. However, it is not the circumcision of the flesh that matters. If you believe that Jesus is the Christ you are born of God (1 John 5:1). You are in His family. It is the circumcision of the heart that God looks at. If you would send us your mailing address we would like to give you a set of tapes.

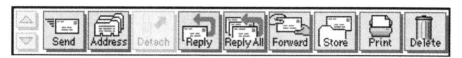

From: scott47@yipee.com
Sent: Saturday, 12 September
To: Audio Book Club (jim@blahblahblah.com)
Subject: order request

Dear Audio Book People:

I am looking for the following books on audiotape:

- Where's Waldo?
- Great Works of Art from the 16th Century
- Colors and Shapes Volume 5
- Sleight of Hand Tricks For Fun and Profit
- Down Yonder: Panoramic Photography from the Southwest
- You're On Your Way To Learning Sign Language
- A Visual History of Corn

Can you please tell me if you have any or all of these books available on audiotape and how much they would be?

Thank you for your time.

Sincerely,

Scott Neumann, Exorcist

From: Jim Recordings <jim@blahblahblah.com>
Sent: Saturday, 12 September
To: scott47@yipee.com
Subject: order request

Sorry, We carry mostly classics. For the books on tape you're requesting, you'll probably find them at *www.booksontape.com*

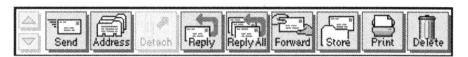

From: scott47@yipee.com
Sent: Friday, 5 June
To: Sock company (suggestions@blahblahblah.com)
Subject: special socks

Dear Sock Manufacturers:

I need your help. While the rest of my leg and foot are quite normal in size, the big toe on my left foot is nearly identical in circumference to the size of Muhammad Ali's head.

Typically, I've simply sliced open the front end of my sock and let my toes hang out the end. Is there a better way? Would it be possible for you to sell me socks with the toe-end sliced open, and a smaller half sock attached to that opening? If the small sock was a size 12, I think that would fit my toe perfectly. I'm looking for a dozen pairs of black, a dozen pairs of argyle, and two dozen pairs of white athletic socks (I play a lot of tennis). Remember the left sock only.

I hope to hear back from you soon.

Sincerely,
Scott Neumann,
President, Pea Growers of American, Eastern Region

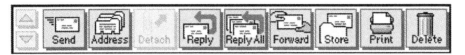

From: Bill@blahblahblah.com
Sent: Monday, 8 June
To: scott47@yipee.com
Subject: question

Thank you for visiting our site. We wish we could help you with your situation but we do not custom order socks. Good luck with your search and should we come across any helpful information we will be sure to email you.

Sincerely,
Bill

From: scott47@yipee.com
Sent: Wednesday, 10 June
To: Sports Company (getfit@blahblahblah.com)
Subject: new product

Dear Exercise Equipment People:

I would like to introduce you to the next revolution in fitness: Toe-X.

Toe-X is a state-of-the-art exercise machine I've invented to help to strengthen the webbing between human toes. With Toe-X, people can tighten that problem area between their digits, reduce cracking and peeling skin, reinforce soft tissue, and have a nice, cushiony place for their toe lint.

In just 11 minutes and 14 seconds a day, your customers will look better, feel stronger, and be more comfortable with their webbing.

Based upon the success of my other exercise machines—the Belly Button Blaster, the Eye Socketizer and the Elbow Burner, I feel confident that Toe-X will be a resounding success.

Orders are filling up fast. I will be happy to send you one at no cost. Join the Toe-X revolution today! It's Webbing Heaven!

Sincerely,
Scott Emily Elizabeth Neumann

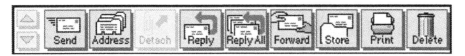

From: getfit@blahblahblah.com
Sent: Thursday, 11 June
To: scott47@yipee.com
Subject: new product

Dear Mr. Neumann:

We had received your email introducing your new exercise machine Toe-X.
Could you kindly send us a picture(s) of your product for our consideration,
we will study it and then we will decide if you should send us the sample.
Thank you very much, hoping to receive your information ASAP.

Freeman Wutu
General Manager-Sports Co. Ltd., Taiwan

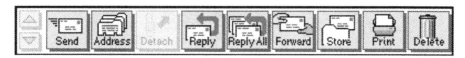

From: scott47@yipee.com
Sent: Friday, June 12,
To: Police Station (gs@blahblahblah.com)
Subject: police assistance

Dear Law Enforcement People:

Hi. I'd like to come down to your station and borrow a radar gun, a police car and an off-duty officer.

You see, the speedometer recently broke on my car. I now have no way of knowing exactly how fast I'm driving. This is what I'm thinking: if my wife rides shotgun in the police car, she can hold the radar gun to let me know my MPH. Then the officer who's driving could count how many rotations of the tire I'm getting per minute, so I'll know exactly how fast I'm going.

I can't see this taking more than an hour.

Sirs, I have an impeccable driving record and I don't want to damage my reputation in any way.

Any day other than next Thursday would be good for me.

Thanks for your time. And keep up the good work. If not for you, there'd be a lot of crazy bad guys running around.

Sincerely,
Scott Neumann, Magnet magnate

From: gs@blahblahblah.com
Sent: Friday, June 12
To:scott47@yipee.com
Subject: assistance

Scott:

Sorry—we like to provide as much police service as possible, but we need to place some limits. In a case like this, we refer people to an auto repair shop.

Chief of Police

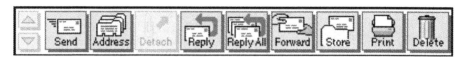

From: scott47@yipee.com
Sent: Wednesday, 10 June
To: Bank (cak@blahblahblah.com)
Subject: money

Dear Banking Person:

I was excited to recently read that your credit union is now accepting Monopoly money at ten cents on the dollar.

Will we have to pass GO before we can convert $200? Also, will we be given actual change or small green houses?

This is much better idea than "a free Shetland pony with every the opening of a new checking account" idea I heard about. I hope to hear back from you soon.

Peace be with you.

Sincerely,

Moyel Scott Neumann

"To me, everyday is 10% off day"

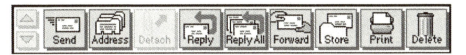

From: cak@blahblahblah.com
Sent: Wednesday, 10 June
To: scott47@yipee.com
Subject: money

Scott:

Just wanted to thank you for visiting our site and let you know that I received your e-mail. I've been on vacation, so I'm not sure I know what you're talking about, but I will check into it.

CAK

From: scott47@yipee.com
Sent: Friday, 14 August
To: Motor Vehicle Dept. (QUESTIONS@dmv.blahblahblah.us)
Subject: parking permit

Dear People In Charge Of Letting People Drive People:

I am interested in purchasing a handicapped parking permit. I'm quite healthy, but I have neither the patience nor the time to drive around looking for a place to park my car. I am busy. Very busy. I am the busiest person I know. My wife always says to me, "I can't believe how busy you are." I say, "I know." Almost every place I go, there are at least 1 or 2 unused handicapped spaces. What a waste! Like those people go shopping.

Please let me know what procedures I need to go through to get my handicapped permit. My next door neighbor Brent Fiorucci would like one, too. He's not busy though, he's just lazy.

Sincerely,

Scott Neumann

Sales Consultant, American International.

"An International Company in America"

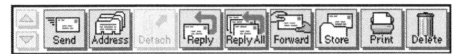

From: QUESTIONS@dmv.blahblahblah.us
Sent: Friday, 14 August
To: scott47@yipee.com
Subject: parking permit

Dear Mr. Neumann:

The Department of Motor Vehicles wishes to thank you for your recent visit to our website. We are pleased to be able to respond to your inquiry. Temporary or permanent parking placards and plates are available for citizens with a temporary disability—physician determines the expected length of the disability or a permanent disability—in their physician's opinion, will not improve. A completed Disabled Parking Placard Application (DL-41) needs to be completed by your physician certifying your disability. The form can be downloaded from the web site. The cost for the placard is $5.00. If I can be of further assistance, please do not hesitate to contact me again.

Sincerely,
Connie
Customer Information Services
Department of Motor Vehicles

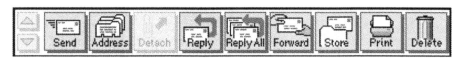

From: scott47@yipee.com
Sent: Friday, 28 August
To: Orchestra (nbfiddle@blahblahblah.com)
Subject: query

Dear Old Tyme Orchestra People:

Y must tell you, Y was so excyted to see your websyte. Y thought Y was the only person left on earth who ys still replacyng the letter "i" with the letter "y". Y do yt yn all of my wrytten communycatyons. Yt's really a lot of fun and people truly get a byg kyck out of yt! Do you know yf there ys some type of "Y" Club? You've now gyven me reason to belyeve that Y'm not the only one around who styll enjoys thys classyc old style. Y hope to hear back from yn the not too dystant future.

Syncerely,

Scott Neumann

A fryend

From: Wilson nbfiddle@blahblahblah.com
Sent: Monday, 31 August
To: scott47@yipee.com
Subject: query

Scott,

No, sorry, we have not hear of a "Y" club. We did chose to use that particular spelling because it does enhance it and keep it original! Good luck
finding a "Y" club.

Wilson

From: scott47@yipee.com
Sent: Wednesday, 21 June
To: Warhol Museum (warhol@blahblahblah.org)
Subject: technicality issue

Dear Andy Warhol Museum People:

I have an acquaintance who was involved in a crime ring that stole over 150 green and tan station wagons over the past 4 years; they then sold the windshield wipers to black market manufacturers in South America. I want you to know that there were no car-jackings, they were all clean thefts from malls, car dealerships, and one from a minister in our church parking lot.

At any rate, the arrest made the local news. I taped it, and timed it, and the story was 2:11 seconds. Hence, my question: did Warhol believe that an individual's fifteen minutes of fame was a cumulative element of time, and if so, would you round it up to the nearest full minute, or would it be held to a more exacting standard? In other words, would my friend now have 12:49 remaining seconds…or 13 minutes exactly? Sirs, I realize my question may seem trivial in light of the circumstances surrounding this situation, but these are the types of things he and I often discussed prior to his incarceration. I look forward to hearing back from you.

Sincerely,
Scott Neumann
East Coast Paper Clip Company, A Division of The United States Paper Clip Company, A Division of The North American Paper Clip Company, a Division of the Spanish Paper Clippo Company.

From: Warhol@blahblahblah.org
Sent: Friday, 23 June 23
To: scott47@yipee.com
Subject: technical issue

Dear Scott:

Thank you for your interest in The Andy Warhol Museum (and your interesting letter).It is believed that Warhol was speaking metaphorically in regards to his quote on 15 minutes of fame. Whether a person has 5, 15, or 30 minutes of fame is less of importance than a person just having their moment in the sun. One of our archivists suggests that you could take the quote literally, meaning your incarcerated acquaintance still has 12:49 remaining to his claim of the high life and high style. But please be aware that this call is not an academic decision, rather an opinion.

From: scott47@yipee.com
Sent: Friday, 30 January
To: Hockey League (ahl@blahblahblah.net)
Subject: my son

Dear League Hockey People:

My son Brent is 19 years old, and I believe he has a future in professional hockey. He is the star goaltender of his Ford plant intramural team. In 17 games, he has not allowed a goal! He is that good.

You should know that aside from quick reflexes, the one thing that enables him to stand out from any other goaltender I've ever seen is his size. He's 8'9" and 585 pounds. (I'm 6'5, 310, my wife is 5'11", weight unknown). Quite frankly, when David has his pads and uniform on, he covers the entire goal. Every once in a while, he has to move a little to the right or left, but that's just to reach for his milkshake bottle on the back of the net. In reality, he pretty much has to stand there and he's got a shutout. His nickname is "The Big Fat Humongous Wall".

Do you know of any teams in your league which are looking for a goaltender? If he tried out, I think they'd be very impressed. And as big as he is, he's a nice boy, too. Other than that one incident with the chemistry teacher and the nitrous oxide, he's never been a problem. He's like a giant teddy bear. On skates.

I hope to hear back from you soon.

Sincerely,
Scott Neumann

A Proud Member of Earth since 1961

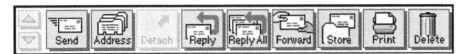

From: ahl@blahblahblah.net
Sent: Friday, 30 June
To: scott47@yipee.com
Subject: your son

Dear Scott,

The players in the AHL are players on contracts with an NHL teams and have been drafted or worked their way up through the various developmental leagues as prospects. The AHL is the hockey equivalent of AAA baseball. Your son would need to secure a try-out with one of the following leagues. These are where players break in and work their way up.

The average player in these leagues makes around $350 a week.

Best of luck
Brian

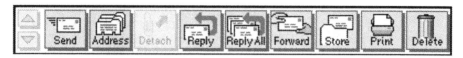

From: scott47@yipee.com
Sent: Wednesday, January 21
To: Dictionary (kwilkes@blahblahblah.com)
Subject: new word

Dear Dictionary People:

I've come up with a word that I think would fit in nicely in the "e"'s section of your dictionary. Most of my friends like it and we use it often during the course of the day, particularly after eating Italian food. I'm a bit uncomfortable revealing the word yet because I haven't had it copyrighted. I also have a little bit of a paranoia problem.

What sort of procedure do I need to go through to get my word in your book? Once we get closer, I'll tell you what it is. I think you'll like the way it sounds.

By the way, my word could also be spelled with a silent "g" if you feel that there are too many "e" words. Thank you.

Sincerely,
Scott Neumann

Tan-O-Matic Tanning Bed Inc.
"You Won't Get Cancer, Or You Next Visit Is Free!"

From: kwilkes@blahblahblah.com
Sent: Thursday, 22 January
To: scott47@yipee.com
Subject: new word

Dear Mr. Neumann:

Thank you for writing us about your word. It sounds like it must be a useful term, and we're glad that you and your friends had the linguistic creativity to invent such a word for yourselves. It is precisely because of innovative efforts like yours that our language continues to grow and change. Before we can enter any word in our dictionaries, however, we must have proof that the word has become established in the language. The best way to get your word in the dictionary, then, is for you to use it and persuade others to do the same. If it catches on, it may eventually turn up in some of the publications we regularly monitor for new words. And, if it turns up often enough, it may even make its way into one or more of our dictionaries. Even if your word never makes it into the dictionary, though, you shouldn't let that deter you from using it. There are many, many words in the English language which are not common enough to appear in the dictionary but are nevertheless useful, legitimate words. If you enjoy using your word, and it serves a purpose for you and your friends, then you should by all means continue to use it. I hope I've been helpful. Good luck with your word.

Sincerely,
K. Wilkes Editorial Department

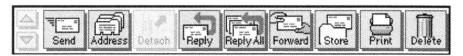

From: scott47@yipee.com
Sent: Friday, 23 January
To: The Kellogg's Company (deanne@blahblahblah.com)
Subject: ad response

Dear Maybe Employer Person:

I saw your ad for a Senior Level Promotions Manager at Kellogg's and thought I'd respond.

I currently work for a major software development company in the Midwest. In the time I've been there, we've experienced tremendous growth and are considering expanding into the South and the Eastern Seaboard.

I want you to know that while I am not our Senior Level Promotion Manager, I do deliver his mail, and based upon what I have seen that he does everyday, I believe I could easily do the job with a minimal amount of training.

I am a college graduate (Miami University, Class of '91—GO RED-SKINS!) and I feel as if I have not yet reached my potential. I am waiting to meet the right person who will realize that I can bring a lot more to a company than just deliver mail or move boxes.

I also have heard that Kalamazoo has a lot of good bars. And I think it would be cool to say, "I live in Kalamazoo." I realize that I may not be the ideal candidate on paper, but I am a hard worker and I have NEVER taken more than an hour for lunch. I think that says a lot about me.

If you would like to see my resume, I can put one together and send it to you. Or if you can offer me any career advice, that would kick ass, too. I look forward to hearing back from you.

Sincerely, Scott "The Weasel" Neumann.

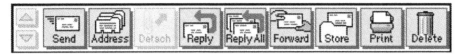

From: deanne@blahblahblah.com
Sent: Monday, 26 January 1998
To: scott47@yipee.com
Subject: thank you

Dear Sir:

Thank you for your interest in employment opportunities with Kellogg Company. We will review your qualifications and job interests and try to match them with our current needs. If there is a position for which you are qualified, we will contact you in the near future. If you are not contacted, please be assured that your resume will be kept on file for a reasonable period of time for future consideration. Again, thank you for your interest in Kellogg Company.

Sincerely, HUMAN RESOURCES

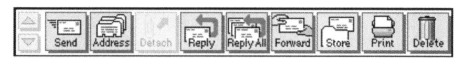

From: scott47@yipee.com
Sent: Tuesday, 17 February
To: Hair Clinic (hairdo@blahblahblah.com)
Subject: ailment

Dear Hair Loss Treatment People:

I have a full, healthy head of hair. But all of my pubic hair is falling out.

It started as just a couple of loose strands, but now, every time I take a shower, I am seeing clumps of curly little brown hairs in the drain. Christ, I'm buying Liquid Plumb'r by the case. If you saw me naked, you'd understand my concern. My groin looks like those crop circles that the aliens leave in the fields over in England. My wife said she doesn't care, but my girlfriend is not very happy.

Have you ever heard of this problem? I'm not sure where to turn anymore. Do they make Scrotum Propecia?

I look forward to hearing back from you.

Sincerely,

Scott Neumann

Sales Rep, American International

"We're Making America International"

From: hairdo@blahblahblah.com
Sent: Wednesday, 18 February
To: scott47@yipee.com
Subject: ailment

Mr. Neumann:

I am sorry, but I have never had a patient with your problem. I have never heard of a patient with such a problem except those who have had radiation treatments or chemotherapy. I am at a loss for advice.

Gods Warmest Blessings,
Carlos

From: scott47@yipee.com
Sent: Tuesday, 17 February
To: Pet Of The Day (kara@blahblahblah.com)
Subject: nomination

Dear Caring Pet People:

I'm interested in nominating my dog as the Pet of the Day. My dog, Nunchucks, is a black lab. We've had him since birth, and he's been an important part of our family for years. He's a great dog. And he's absolutely beautiful. Unfortunately, he's also dead.

He got loose about 3 and a half weeks ago. He started chasing the mailman, and then the mailman panicked and ran into a kid on a skateboard, and then the skateboard flipped into the street, and a car swerved out of the way to miss the skateboard and instead hit a garbage can which rolled towards Nunchucks, who jumped to avoid it and he fell into an open man hole.

The experience has been horrible. We've lost a member of the family. And my kids really missed the smell of his urine on the carpet.

Ma'am, can a deceased animal be nominated for Pet of the Day? This is one of those times in life when you wish you had done something and now it's too late. (I never got to tell my grandfather how much I admired his teeth, either.) I realize the award may be posthumous, but I think it would help our family through the grieving process.

Thank you for your time.

Sincerely,
Scott Neumann
Devoted Father, Loving Husband, Dead Dog Owner

From: kara@blahblahblah.com
Sent: Wednesday, 18 February
To: scott47@yipee.com
Subject: pet nomination

Dear Scott:

Thank you for your interest in Pet of the Day. What an odd and tragic way to lose a family member and friend. Poor Nunchucks. It is absolutely possible for an animal to be Pet of the day posthumously. We have had several, including a Black Lab.

I hope this helps. Kara

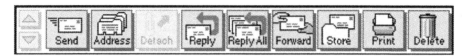

From: scott47@yipee.com
Sent: Wednesday, 18 February
To: Baseball Card printers (info@blahblahblah.com)
Subject: kids

Dear Baseball Card Printing People:

I am the coach of the little league baseball team for juvenile delinquents. It was rough at first. The kids stole food and money from the concession stand, smashed their bats into the umpires, and at least once a game, somebody shot a pigeon in the outfield.

Things are slightly better now, but I'm thinking that if we create a series of baseball cards for our players, it would help to build up their self-esteem. I wrote a sample card for one of our players:

FRONT OF THE CARD: Brent Fiorucci, Third Baseman, A-1 Check Cashing.

BACK OF THE CARD: 9 years old Brent now utilizes his God-given speed to run the bases instead of from the cops. Two years ago, Brent had 3 breaking and entering convictions on his record; last year Brent hit .350, showing a grace with the bat that was once limited to a saw-off shotgun.

I think these could really help. Do you people write these, or should I? If you could please let me know what type of information I need to provide to you. Thank you for your time.

Sincerely,
Scott Neumann

P.S. Our team is now 12-0. All twelve wins have been by forfeit. Our players celebrate every victory by setting the dugout on fire.

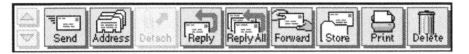

From: info@blahblahblah.com
Sent: Thursday, 19 February
To: scott47@yipee.com
Subject: kids

Hi Scott:

You obviously had your hands full for the past 6 months. I can see you've kept your sense of humor through it all. I'm sure that it is no easy task to work with kids that have grown up not knowing that everyone doesn't steal and beat each other up. Thankfully there are people like you that are willing to help make the world a better place to live and give these kids a chance. We can do the cards you asked about. We have an order form on our website or I can send you some. Also if you can let me know how many kids you want to do this for I will quote you a different price than what is listed. One thing we have found in doing Trading Cards is that all kids like seeing themselves on them. Especially if you can get someone to take pictures during the game. (that might not be easy). Please feel free to call our toll free number if you have any more questions.

Best Regards, Pam

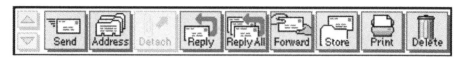

From: scott47@yipee.com
Sent: Friday, 30 January
To: Weight Doctor (drken@blahblahblah.net)
Subject: joint venture?

Dear Doctor That Helps Fat People Person:

I'm 5'10, 95 pounds. I'm thin. Very thin. I've always been thin. The only weight problem I have is that I need to gain weight. I can eat as much as I want and never gain an ounce. I don't exercise. I haven't exercised since grade school. If you call throwing rocks at windows and running away, exercise.

I have a voracious appetite, too. This is what I had for breakfast today: a bagel with cream cheese and butter, 6 fried eggs, 3 slices of bacon, a frozen waffle, a large glass of orange juice, coffee, four pieces of chocolate cake and a cherry danish!

At any rate, I'm thinking about going into motivational speaking. People say I can be quite dynamic and that I really know how to light a fire. I thought that a good place to start would be as a person who speaks to overweight people. Like your clients. I mean, if they can see me...hear about my lifestyle...how sedentary I am...how I can literally devour a refrigerator...and everything else I can do because I'm thin, maybe they'll be inspired to lose weight and be like me!!!

I'm really excited about this idea. I think I could really help some of your big, fat clients.

Sincerely, Scott Neumann

Author: "Reading Lips: The Key To Small Business Success"

P.S. I just ordered three small pizzas for lunch. I bet I'll lose three pounds.

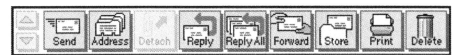

From: drken@blahblahblah.net
Sent: Monday, 2 February
To: scott47@yipee.com
Subject: joint venture?

Scott:

Fat people like myself resent genetically thin people like yourself. You would find a very difficult audience. Dr. Michael Weintraub in his original paper describing the benefits of phen-fen said one of the things they learned from their original study was that patients resented the way normal weight dieticians talked to them. You almost have to have been there to know how to talk with fat people. Your diet doesn't sound any too healthful. Have you had your triglycerides and HDL & LDL cholesterol checked? Thin people can have heart attacks.
Incidentally, I have never seen a thin person like yourself gain weight. Just thank your lucky stars.

Ken M.D.

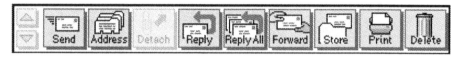

From: scott47@yipee.com
Sent: Sunday, 15 February
To: Business Advice (lips@blahblahblah.com)
Subject: new business venture

Dear New Business Assistance People:

I have a restaurant idea that I feel would work well in today's market-place: "Gefilt-O-Fast", the fast, fresh gefilte fish alternative. You can eat-in or take out....there would be a wide variety of flavors including traditional, chicken, and macaroni and cheese. I also plan on offering "Gefildessert", which could be jello molds or pieces of cake shaped liked gefilte fish.

I believe that in today's society, more and more people are expanding their ethnic diversity and are willing to try foods from other cultures—witness the explosive growth of pierogies, kielbasa, and french toast. We all know how mainstream bagels have become, and it is my belief that the next great Jewish food will be gefilte fish.

I eagerly look for your response to see if I should move ahead with my idea.

Sincerely,

Scott Neumann

P.S. My other idea is the "Iraq of Lamb Shoppe".

From: lips@blahblahblah.com
Sent: Sunday, 15 February
To: scott47@yipee.com
Subject: answer

Sir:

Gefilte fish is not exactly a mainstream item. I can't see anyone building a whole concept around it. Good Luck. You'll need it.

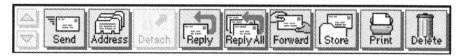

From: scott47@yipee.com
Sent: Tuesday, 3 February
To: Pharmacist (hack@blahblahblah.com)
Subject: dosage ?

Dear Pharmacists People:

I am currently taking Nasaqort AQ and twenty or forty other over-the-counter medications for my allergies. I was told to not operate heavy machinery.

My question is this: I drive to work everyday. We have two cars: a Jeep Cherokee and a Honda Civic. I called the dealerships and the weight of the Civic is significantly less than the Jeep. Does that mean it's safe for me to drive the Honda to work? Or should I not got at all? My boss wouldn't be too happy about that, but doctor's orders are doctor's order, right? I sure could use a few days off, anyway. To be safe, I'm having my brother-in-law drive me today. And he's an alcoholic.

I hope to hear back from you tomorrow.

Sincerely,
Scott Neumann

Receptionist, American International

"An International Company in America"

From: hack@blahblahblah.com
Sent: Friday, 6 February
To: scott47@yipee.com
Subject: response

Mr. Neumann:

The reason that your doctor told you not to operate heavy machinery is due to the side effects associated with the drugs you are taking. These include dizziness and drowsiness. I am assuming that you just started on some of these medications. Your doctor wants you to get a good idea of how these drugs affect you before you take a chance and drive your car or operate a crane, etc…I would suggest you take the bus to work for at least a week. This will give you time to learn if you will be significantly affected by these drugs. If you don't have any side effects that would alter your ability to operate heavy machinery safely, then you can drive to work.

Thank you, C. Hack

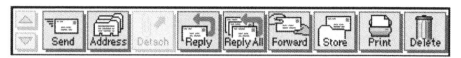

From: scott47@yipee.com
Sent: Friday, 13 March
To: TV News station (dparks@blahblahblah.com)
Subject: job opening

Dear Television Station People:

I would like to apply for the position of weatherman. Although I have no formal experience or training, I have what I believe to be a natural instinct to determine upcoming weather.

Ever since I was a child, my body signals me when certain weather conditions occur. For example, when a cold front is coming, my left foot starts shaking severely. Or when thunder is in the area, I feel a tremendous craving for tuna fish. I also have the ability to walk outside and instantly tell the exact temperature by rubbing my hand on a maple tree while whistling "Oh Susannah." And I'm never wrong.

How can we set up an interview? Can I just come down and give the weather a shot for a couple of days? Tomorrow's bad, though. There's going to be a big thunderstorm—just kidding! I hope to hear back from you soon.

Sincerely,

Scott Neumann

P.S. I think I would be really good at chitchatting at the end of the news, too. I know a lot of good jokes!

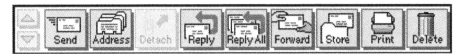

From: dparks@blahblahblah.com
Sent: Friday, 13 March
To: scott47@yipee.com
Subject: openings

Hello Scott...All current job openings are listed on our website's employment page. Unfortunately for you, we are not looking for weather talent such as yourself at this time. It's true that some people have a natural gift for things. You are the first I've ever heard of that has one for weather. Good luck in your search.

D. Parks

From: scott47@yipee.com
Sent: Thursday, 12 November
To: Mime School (savi@blahblahblah.com)
Subject: career advice

Dear Mime School People:

   I recently had laryngitis for about a week, and I was forced to communicate with people through hand signals and facial gestures. I received many, many compliments at the office about my ability to get my point across by "acting out" my words. I am also very, very good at charades. As such, I am now contemplating a career change to "mime". I realize that miming is a radical departure from pork futures, but I think I've got "it". How much could a good mime make?

   Any information you can provide me with about your program would be appreciated. I look forward to hearing back from you soon. Well, hearing from you in the metaphorical sense.

Sincerely,
Scott Neumann
(Imagine that I'm mime-waving goodbye)

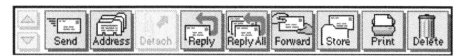

From: savi@blahblahblah.com
Sent: Friday, 13 November
To: scott47@yipee.com
Subject: advice

Hello Scott Newman:

Thank you for your words and your willing to know more about this beautiful art of total expression and honesty of integrating body and mind. It's very good that you want to become a mime. It takes years, and good teachers, plus many other things.
Thank you again for your sincere approach to ask for info and share your aspirations with me. You are really a daring person to want to change careers with an art that is not much appreciated in the USA. Bravo ! Bon courage.

Warmly yours,
Samuel

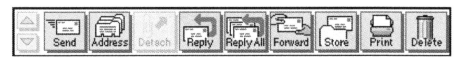

From: scott47@yipee.com
Sent: Friday, 21 August
To: Eyeglass Store (grants@blahblahblah.com)
Subject: glasses

Dear Eyecare People:

I am unbelievably nearsighted. I am actually typing this with my nose because if my face is more than a quarter of an inch away from the keypad, I can't see the letters. I broke my glasses late last night when a bee landed on my forehead while I was watching "Green Acres", and when I tried to kill it with the phone book, I missed, hit my forehead and smashed my left lens. I am so fucking annoyed. Unfortunately, my doctor is on vacation in Bermuda for the next two weeks. Bastard. Anyway, I had to take the day off of work today. It would be impossible for me to dissect micro antibodies in this condition. Frankly, it took me 3 hours to find my computer in the house. I started typing this letter on the microwave.

I'd like to schedule an appointment with the next two days. I really need some new glasses soon.

Christ, I don't know how Helen Keller did it.

Sincerely,

Senator Scott Neumann

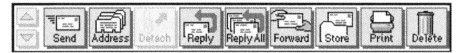

From: grants@blahblahblah.com
Sent: Friday, 23 October
To: scott47@yipee.com
Subject: response

Dear Scott:

We have some computer problems as of late and have just gotten them sorted out. You have probably gotten some new glasses already but there will be a next time for your eyecare needs. We know it.

Please understand Scott, our #1 goal in all that we do is to help out customers look their best and see great! Although it's taken us over two months to respond, rest assured, nobody is faster to serve than we are!

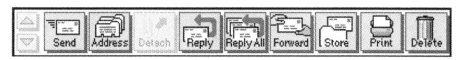

From: scott47@yipee.com
Sent: Monday, 12 October
To: Balloon Store (staff@blahblahblah.com)
Subject: gift order

Dear Balloon Gift Sending People:

I would like to place an order for a bouquet of balloons to be sent as a birthday present. This is what I would like the card to read:

"Dear Cathy:

You're more than just my father's-aunt's-sister's-dad's-brother's-uncle's-second cousin's-sister-in-law, you're somebody really special. Happy Milestone Birthday. I can't believe you're 41 1/2! "

Love, Scott

She lives in Buffalo, New York. What would you recommend I send and how much would this cost?

Thanks for your time.

Sincerely,
Scott Neumann
C.H.J.K.U.U.T.P.O.Q.X.R.T.V. Enterprises

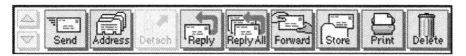

From: staff@blahblahblah.com
Sent: Monday, 12 October
To: scott47@yipee.com
Subject: gift order

SCOTT:

FOR BALLOONS DELIVERED IN BUFFALO NEW YORK PLEASE CALL: BALLOONS OVER BUFFALO AT BLAHBLAHBLAH AND ASK FOR EXT.22 THIS WAY YOU GET LOCAL PRICES AND PRODUCT CHOICES AVAILABLE. AND HAPPY BIRTHDAY TO YOUR RELATIVE!

From: scott47@yipee.com
Sent: Friday, 16 October
To: Clerk Of Courts (Tfreeberg@blahblahblah.net)
Subject: assistance required

Dear Official Documents Person:

I am writing to request information on changing my date of birth.

I was born on March 4, 1961. However, many good things have happened to me on July 16. On July 16, 1987, I found a $20 bill at a bus stop. On July 16, 1979, I met Hank Aaron in a restroom at the airport. On July 16, 1992, my close friend Brent Fiorucci was bit by a dog and I wasn't. Due to these events and many others, I would like to officially make July 16 my birthday. Please let me know what paperwork I need to fill out and how much this will cost.

I hope to get this done ASAP because March 4 is right around the corner and I need to let my family know so they won't send a card and then be embarrassed when I tell them that my birthday is longer March 4, but July 16.

Sincerely,

Scott Neumann
D.O.B. 7/16/61—-soon!

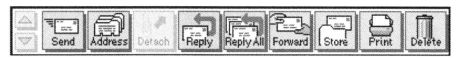

From: Tfreeberg@blahblahblah.net
Sent: Friday, 16 October
To: scott47@yipee.com
Subject: assistance

Dear Mr. Neumann:

In response to your request for information on changing your date of birth, I must inform you that a person's date of birth cannot be changed. If you are in need of further assistance, you may contact Vital Records.

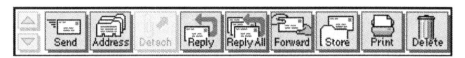

From: scott47@yipee.com
Sent: Monday, 19 October
To: Office Supplies (databank@blahblahblah.net)
Subject: office supplies

Dear People To Order Office Products From People:

I am looking for the following office supplies:
*5 dozen left-hand pencils
*6 foot thick legal pads (yellow only)
*4 reams of plaid paper
*a desktop calendar for the year 1954
*a box of battery-operated thumbtacks
*one carton of lickable sticky notes

   Please let me know the total cost and also how much it would be for delivery. My litmus paper manufacturing business is in Buffalo, New York. Thank your for your time. I hope to hear back from soon.

Sincerely,

Scott Neumann

Manufacturing Division, American International

"Internationally Known In America"

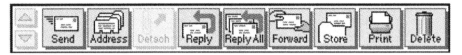

From: daisy chang<databank@blahblahblah.net
Sent: Wednesday, 21 October
To: scott47@yipee.com
Subject: office supplies

Dear Mr. Neumann,

Thanks for your e-mail. We are sorry that we can't offer you products as you mentioned in your e-mail because they are no longer available.
In case you are interested in any one of our other products, please don't hesitate to let us know. Looking forward to receiving your further message!!

Best Regards,

DAISY CHANG/EXPORT DEPT.

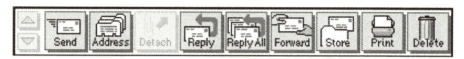

From: scott47@yipee.com
Sent: Tuesday, 1 September
To: Motel (Kan@blahblahblah.com)
Subject: complaint

Dear Motel People Who Made Me Really Mad People:

I recently stayed at your motel, and I must tell you, it was tinkubop horrible! Where the wasgsrad do you people get off having rooms that are so bundrezingly dirty that it looked like a vilming pig crisutf! I was so grasfuros embarrassed when my wife walked in the room I thought she was going to cerwus her pants! Sirs, normally, I am a calm, sane, rational human being. But I've stayed at a lot of hotels and motels in my day, and yours was one of the pinbefaw othanush worst!

You should be embarrassed. Normally I would expect some sort of reimbursement from a quality chain, but you people are a bunch of worthless wazgibs.

Sincerely, Scott Neumann

P.S. One more thing. I think the name of your ghuccab motel sucks! You probably thought of it yourself, you itudally humodgranks, you.

From: Kan@blahblahblah.com
Sent: Tuesday 1 September
To: scott47@yipee.com
Subject: stay

Dear Mr. Dirtbag:

If the room you stayed in was such a mess and dirty it had to occur the minute you walked your stinking body through the door, you scum bag. I wouldn't give a penny back, you can't prove you stayed here and we probably wouldn't have rented to a Mongoloid like you. F-you.

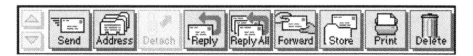

From: scott47@yipee.com
Sent: Wednesday 2 September
To: Office Of Rare Diseases (sgb@blahblahblah.com)
Subject: disease notification

Dear Rare Disease Listing People:

I was in your site and my God, I had no idea there were that many rare diseases found throughout the world! However, I did notice that my ailment was not listed. I am currently in the secondary stages of Tubble-Oismondilitis. As I'm sure you know, Tubble-Oismondilitis causes fluorescent green ear wax, an excessively long left eyebrow, and the inability to say the word "pirate". As best as I can tell, there is only one other known case of Tubble-Oismondilitis is the United States. His name is Brent Fiorucci and he lives in Jacksonville. I've never met him. But I've heard he's got the earwax really bad. I thought it was important for you to add Tubble-Oismondilitis to your list because there may be someone else out there whose belly button is leaking puss and they don't have a clue what it is. They need to know that it's Tubble-Oismondilitis. I hope to hear back from you soon that Tubble-Oismondilitis will now be included in your site.

    You are very informative people!

Sincerely,
Scott Neumann

P.S. I know someone who has Wegener's Granulamotosis.

From: sgb@blahblahblah.com
Sent: Friday, 4 September
To: scott47@yipee.com
Subject: response

Sir:

Thank you for contacting the Office of Rare Diseases at the National Institutes of Health through our Web Site. We are unable to add specific diseases such as yours to our list unless we have documented cases on file. If you need further assistance, please feel free to contact the Office and include your postal mailing address and telephone number in the message. Thank you for your inquiry.

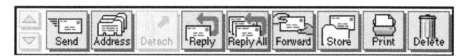

From: scott47@yipeemail.com
Sent: Wednesday, 2 September
To: Pediatrician (chitka@blahblahblah.com)
Subject: medical issue

Dear Professional Know-Everything-About-Kids People:

   Our newborn girl hates the taste of baby formula. But she loves lique-fied bison meat. Does this pose any type of long-term health problem? She seems to be progressing nicely and growing quite well, but my wife still gets a bit unnerved when she's the only one at her playgroup who has to puree a buffalo steak. Also, bison must be extremely acidic because my wife's nipples really burn quite a bit. This doesn't seem like a good sign to me. But you're the experts. I hope to hear back from you soon.

Sincerely,

Scott Neumann

Marketing Director, Bonifide Centerior Developers, or if you don't have a lot of time, BCD.

From: chitka@blahblahblah.com
Sent: Wednesday, 2 September
To: scott47@yipeemail.com
Subject: response

Dear Mr. Scott:

Thanks for the query but I must admit a very unusual one. I am surprised as to why the newborn baby is not on exclusive breast-feeding. If there have been compelling reasons not to breast feed, there are so many infant milk formulas available which differ in taste & flavor and if you had persisted with any of them the baby would have certainly started accepting. Out of all the things available in the world you decided to put your child on buffalo meat puree speaks of your perverted attitude. All effort is made to humanize various baby formulas to bring it closest to breast milk yet you decided to animalize the child by feeding her bison meat. Such practice not only exposes the child to obnoxious foreign proteins but also stresses the tender kidneys & the liver and can result in many difficult medical problems in the child. It is still not too late. Consult your pediatrician to select a safer substitute which the child will relish.

Regards, Dr.A. Chitka, MD

From: scott47@yipee.com
Sent: Monday, 14 September
To: PR Firm (firman@blahblahblah.com)
Subject: exciting news!

Dear Public Relations Professional Person:

I am contacting quality firms such as yours across the country to let you know about a remarkable public relations opportunity for you and your clients. I represent a man named Brent Fiorucci who has been traveling across Europe for three years billed as "The King Of Hunger Strikes."

From Prague to Dublin to Cannes, Mr. Fiorucci has wowed crowds with his remarkable ability to go for 10-31 days without food. And now, he's coming to a city near you! We believe that Mr. Fiorucci's talent for starvation can be utilized in ways that may benefit all of us. As such, we are offering you the opportunity to have Mr. Fiorucci's next hunger strike take place in front of one of your client's corporate offices. Over the past three years, Mr. Fiorucci has performed dozens of hunger strikes, and gained and lost hundreds of pounds. The true beauty, however, is that every single time he makes a public appearance, the press is waiting. En masse.

Imagine…two full weeks of national media coverage of a man starving himself to death…AND your client's building with its nice big logo strategically situated over his left shoulder.

Sir, it worked in the Alps and it can work for you. Mr. Fiorucci will be making his way to the US in mid-November. He is currently recovering from a 22 day StarvFest at Euro Disney (and ticket sales were up 13% by the way!).

I would welcome the opportunity to send you a press kit on this PR dream come true. I hope hear back from you soon.

Sincerely,

Scott Neumann
Senior Agent, Really Talented Persons

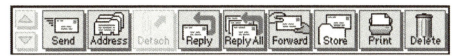

From: firman@blahblahblah.com
Sent: Monday, 14 September
To: scott47@yipee.com
Subject: none

Sir:

I find it incredibly offensive that you would even consider representing someone like this. We can handle our own clients, thank you. Please remove us from your list.

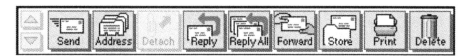

From: scott47@yipee.com
Sent: Friday, 18 September
To: Product Suppliers (tcla@blahblahblah.com)
Subject: success story

Dear Junk Product People (You Know What I Mean):

Like any small businessman, I am always seeking new ways to generate greater traffic patterns in our toilet supply store. I believe we've been pretty creative and we've found some non-traditional approaches, one of which I'd like to share with you.

Last November, we held our first annual Marine Corps Birthday Sale by having an actual Marine corpse in the store. His name was Brent Fiorucci, and he had died a week prior in some sort of target-practice argument. Regardless, his family gave us permission to put this hero on display in his casket and we had a huge turnout! Many people had never been that close to a war hero before, and while they we're looking, it was impossible for them not to notice that we had 10–40% off everything in the store-toilet seats, bulk toilet paper, toilet brushes, and our exclusive Diarrhea De-Scenter. What was once considered a slow week showed revenue increases of 88%!

This year, I'm thinking about doing something in November revolving around Tourette's Syndrome. When people come up to the sales associates and ask how much something is, we could just swear at them and then give them a great discount. I'm going to call it "The Great Fucking Discount Sale". I've got a good feeling about it.

Thanks for your site. Keep up the good work.

Sincerely,

Scott Neumann, Owner, Everything Butt

From: tcla@blahblahblah.com
Sent: Monday, 21 September
To: scott47@yipee.com
Subject: info

Dear Scott:

Recently we have included imprinted toilet paper as a new item in our line of promotional products and thought you may be interested. Please come visit our web page and under the Product Search Engine, search for toilet paper. Please don't hesitate to call us if you have any questions.

Sincerely, Terri, Graphics Inc.

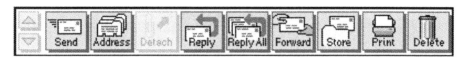

From: scott47@yipee.com
Sent: Friday, 25 September
To: Computer Repair (miller@blahblahblah.com)
Subject: !!!!!!!!!!!

Dear Computer Repair People:

I really need your help. My keyboard
keeeeeeeeeeeeppppppppppppppppppppppssssssssssssssssss
tttttttttttttttttiiiiiiiiiiiiiiiiickiiiiiiiiiiiiiinnnnnnnnnnnnnnnnnng
onnnnnnnnnnnnnnnnnnnnn
mmmmmmmmmmmeeeeeeeeeeeeeeeeeeeeeeeeeeeeeeeeeeeeeeee…
IIIIIIIIIIIIIIIIIIIIIII hhhhhhhave aaaaaaaaaaaaaaaaaaaa
MMMMaacccccccccccciiiiiiiiiiiiiiiiiiiiiiiiiiiiinnnnnnnnntoooosssssssssssshhh
PPPPoweeeeeeeerrrrrrbooookkkkkkkkkkkkkkkkkkkkkkkkkkkkkkkk 5300.
WWWWWWWWWWWWWWWWhennnnnnnnnnnnnnnn
caaaaaaaaaaaaaaaaaaaaaaaaaaaaaaaaannnnnnnnn IIIIIIIIIIIIIIIIIIIIII bring
iiiiiiiiiiiiiiiiiiiiitt in????????????????????????
TTTTTTTTTThhhhhhhhhheeeeeee
ssssssssooooooooooooonnnnnnnnnner theeeeee
bettttttttttteeeerrrrrrrrrrrrrrrrrrrrrrrrrrrrrrrrrr.

Sincccccerellllllllllllllllyyyyyyyyy,

ScottttttttttttttttttttttttttttttNeeeeeeeeuuuuuuuuuuuuuuuuuuuumaaaan

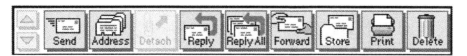

From: miller@blahblahblah.com
Sent: Friday, 25 September
To: scott47@yipee.com
Subject: REPAIR

Scott:

You can bring your laptop in any weekday between the hours of 10am and 3pm. If you need directions to our office, or if these hours are not convenient for you, feel free to call us.

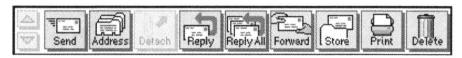

From: scott47@yipee.com
Sent: Friday, 25 September
To: Recording Studio (voicetrack@blahblahblah.com)
Subject: question

Dear Recording Studio Person:

Do you have the technical capabilities to make me sound like a female aardvark?

I am a local zoologist who is in the midst of a 4-year government-funded study examining mating rituals of ungulate mammals. I have been with this particular aardvark, Brent Fiorucci, since birth. I believe he has grown quite attached to me, as I have to him. (Yes, this typically is considered taboo in my field; one should never develop a relationship with a study animal.)

At any rate, he is now 2 1/2 years old, and is about to enter the prime mating period of his life. This is a critical point in our study. Since I have become quite proficient with the language of aardvarks, I feel that if I could go into your studio and modulate my voice to sound like a female companion, I would be able to enter our study chamber with him…play the tape…and witness firsthand how he reacts to a "woman".

My only fear is that he may be a little too aggressive for me in his aroused state. Although I've done studies like this before, and I've never had to make love to an animal. Yet.

Sir, this could prove to be outstanding fact-finding for both our study as well as concurrent mammal research. Please let me know as soon as you can if you have these capabilities.

I look forward to hearing back from you and to your possible involvement in this exciting project.

Sincerely, Scott Neumann
Associate Professor of Zooastronological Studies, Gexzddddrquloqua Community College, Suburban Branch

From: voicetrack@blahblahblah.com
Sent: Friday, 25 September
To: scott47@yipee.com
Subject: question

Hi, Scott

Sounds interesting. We can only alter voice in such a way as to pitch it up or down. We can make you sound younger or older, "chipmunked" or the other extreme (way low). We can thin your voice, thicken it, reverb or delay it, etc. But that's about it. Not sure how any of those might attract an aardvark.

Joel

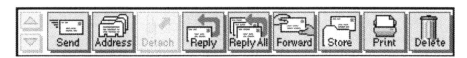

From: scott47@yipee.com
Sent: Monday, 31 August
To: Car Audio Equipment (sounds@blahblahblah.com)
Subject: system errors

Dear Stereo People:

I believe there is something wrong with the automotive stereo system I purchased from your company.

Every time I put a CD in, the front left tire of my car falls off. It happened four times. I explained this to the people at the store and they gave me a new one. Now when I put in a cassette, the garage doesn't open and I get a severe shock in my lower gums. Has anyone else experienced similar problems?

I hope to hear back from you soon. I really miss listening to my Amish chanting tapes.

Sincerely,

Scott Neumann,

Kentucky Speed Dialing Champion, 1990-94

From: sounds@blahblahblah.com
Sent: Monday, 31 August
To: scott47@yipee.com
Subject: errors

Sir:

I have seen this problem before on several occasions. It is generally caused by a "loose nut behind the volume control".

Mike

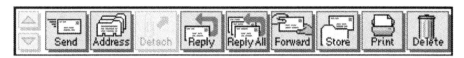

From: scott47@yipee.com
Sent: Monday, 17 August
To: Erotic Entertainment (webmaster@blahblahblah.com)
Subject: photo

Dear XXX Pornographic People:

I have a question about one of the photos in your website. The one in particular I'm referring to is where the blonde woman is wearing the lacy teddy and the patterned thigh-high stocking and has her legs spread wide open, exposing her vagina. Could you please tell me where you bought that lamp on the table behind her? My wife and I have been looking for something like that for quite some time. It would perfectly match the decor of our living room. I hope to hear back from you soon. Thank you in advance for your help.

Sincerely,

Cantor Scott Neumann

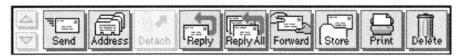

From: webmaster@blahblahblah.com
Sent: Monday, 17 August
To: scott47@yipee.com
Subject: photo

Dear Scott:

Unfortunately, I have no further info on that pic. I was provided by a photographer who I am no longer able to contact. Sorry that I couldn't be of more assistance.

Yours, John

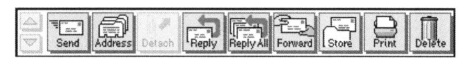

From: scott47@yipee.com
Sent: Thursday, 6 August
To: Census Bureau (wyn@blahblahblah.gov)
Subject: information request

Dear Education Statistics People:

I'm doing a research study titled "The Negative Psychological Effects Of Dental Retainers, Blinking, and Pastel-Colored Styrofoam on High School Students in Eleventh Grade Named Ollie Who Have Pet Goldfish And Wear Size 10 Shoes Or Less."

Do you have any type of statistical evidence that I would be able to use in my study? You will receive full credit for any information you can provide me with.

I hope to hear back from you soon.

Sincerely, Scott Neumann

Author, "Famous African American Yachtsmen"

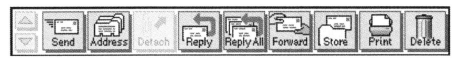

From: wyn@blahblahblah.gov
Sent: Thursday, 6 August
To: scott47@yipee.com
Subject: request

Sir:

The Census Bureau does not collect the information you requested. The National Center for Education Statistics may be able to help you.

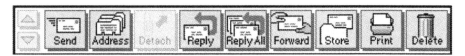

From: scott47@yipee.com
Sent: Thursday, 27 August
To: Song Analysts (dken@blahblahblah.com)
Subject: advice

Dear Song Analysis People:

I was in your website and it's very nice of you to assist upcoming artists in their quest to break into the music industry.

At any rate, I am close to finishing writing what I believe could be a major hit throughout the continental United States. I've never been to Alaska or Hawaii so I don't feel that I can fairly comment on their taste levels. The name of the song is "Pilo's Silo". It's all instrumental—mostly piano and winds, and goes something like this:

La lala lalala lala…LA LA la…LA LA la…LA LA la…Ohhhh, oh oh oh oh Hmmmmmmmm….oh oh oh ….hmmmmmmmm…oh oh oh Doooooooooooooooo……aaaaaYYYYYYYYYYYYYYYaaaaaaaa..Shahahaha ha….Shahahahaha….
FleeeeeeeeeeeeeeeeeeeeeeeeeeeeeeeeeeeeeeeeeeeeeeeeEeeeeeeeeeeeeeeeeeeeeeeee eeeeeeeeeeeEeeeeeeeeeeeeeeeeeeeeeeeeeeeee

CHORUS: THREE PEOPLE HUMMING. A BARKING DOG. AND THEN A FLUTTERING KITE.

This is just the first stanza, but I think you get the idea. Sirs, I am a musician and not a marketer. How do I go about selling this song? I think it will have mass appeal. And I don't mean in the church sense. Christ, I haven't been to church in years.

Sincerely,
Scott Neumann

p.s. Do you happen to have Kenny Roger's phone number?

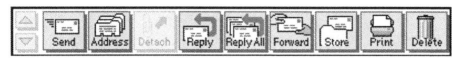

From:dken@blahblahblah.com
Sent: Thursday, 27 August
To: scott47@yipee.com
Subject: song

Scott:

You lost me! If you're sending this type of e-mail out to people who may listen to your stuff then they will not take you seriously. Instrumentals are real, real difficult to shop!

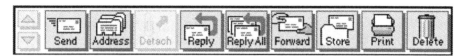

From: scott47@yipee.com
Sent: Tuesday, 25 August
To: Marine Recruiting (f11@blahblahblah.edu)
Subject: applicant

Dear Tough Marine People:

I am interested in purchasing a four-week boot camp gift certificate for my nephew, Brent Fiorucci.

I truly believe Brent is "Marine Material" and he'll benefit from the experience, but I think we all want to make sure he likes it a lot before he commits. Sirs, will he be in with the regulars, or would it be possible if he stayed with his parents at a nearby hotel? He sure does love his cable tv. Please let me know the cost and what time slots are available. His family is planning a ski trip to Austria in October and I'm hoping that you can squeeze him in before they go. Thank you in advance for your help.

Sincerely, Scott Neumann
Army! Navy! Air Force! Marines!

From: f11@blahblahblah.edu
Sent: Wednesday, 26 August
To: scott47@yipee.com
Subject: applicant

Sir:

Your request makes no sense to me. Gift certificates? I have absolutely no idea what you are talking about.

From: scott47@yipee.com
Sent: Monday, 17 August
To: National Football League (NFLQUEST@blahblahblah.com)
Subject: ideas

Dear National Football League People:

I've been a big fan of the NFL for years, and the more I watch, the more I realize that there's really no reason for your players to wear pants. Rest assured, I'm not talking about nude players. What I have in mind is for them to wear kind of a bikini brief with the team logo on the back. Personally, I think most people would be impressed with the size of the leg muscles of these world-class athletes. I know I would be.

"No pants" is just one of hundreds of ideas I have to help to improve the quality of the game in the National Football League. Another is a head coach staring contest.

I'd love to come down to your offices and tell you my thoughts. Thursdays are usually a good day for me. I hope to hear back from you soon.

Sincerely,

Scott Neumann

Go Sabres!

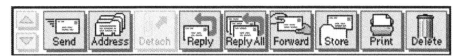

From: NFLQUEST@blahblahblah.com
Sent: Monday, 17 August
To: scott47@yipee.com
Subject: ideas

Dear NFL Fan:

Thank you for contacting us. Your comments and questions are very important. Although we may not respond personally to every inquiry, we value your input and read every comment to constantly improve our quality of service. We hope you will continue to enjoy the many fine features we have to offer.

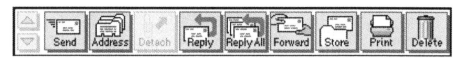

From: scott47@yipee.com
Sent: Thursday, 20 August
To: Law Practice (ba@blahblahblah.com)
Subject: legal help

Dear People I Hope Can Help Me People:

I was visiting your website and you seem to have a lot of experience in family law. I hope so. I've recently split up with my girlfriend of 11 years after she gave birth to our son. It's a long, drawn-out story that I don't really want to get into. Let's just say she's found another "person" she'd rather be with.

At any rate, I discovered earlier this week that she named our little boy Mdcxrrwxqa. Sir, I feel that I have a right to be involved in the final naming decision. I also liked the name Losigyithawc a lot better. Please advise me regarding this situation ASAP. I would like to have this resolved before he gets used to the name Mdcxrrwxqa.

Sincerely,
Scott Neumann
Owner, Hank's Bakery and Fish Shop

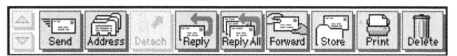

From: ba@blahblahblah.com
Sent: Friday, 29 August
To: scott47@yipee.com
Subject: aid

Scott:

I've handled cases like this before. Call my office and make an appointment. I will give you a free in-person consultation.

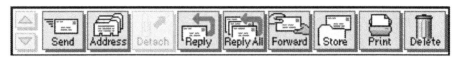

From: scott47@yipee.com
Sent: Friday, 21 August
To: Human Resources (careers@blahblahblah net)
Subject: resume submission

Dear Employee-Seeking People:

I would like to apply for a position with your company. Any job other that doesn't involve learning a foreign language would be fine. As you can see from my resume, I have an extensive background, and I believe I would be as much of as asset to your company as I am to my family.

RESUME:

Name: Scott Neumann

WORK EXPERIENCE:

10/96-present: manager, Acme Sporting Goods. Fired for stealing.
8/96-10/96: assistant night manager, Dawn's Women's Clothing. Fired for drilling a peephole in the changing room.
7/2/96@11 AM-7/2/96@12:30 PM: stock boy, Grocer's Grocery. Fired for telling a customer to "Go fuck yourself."
7/95-7/96: inmate, Restin Correctional Facility.
6/94-7/95: security, the Broward Building. Fired for doing my boss's wife.

If there's anything else you need from me, please don't hesitate to ask. I'm very excited about having the opportunity to work with you.

Sincerely,

Scott Neumann

p.s. If you need a reference, I can give you the number of my parole officer.

From: careers@blahblahblah.net
Sent: Wednesday, 26 August
To: scott47@yipee.com
Subject: resume

Dear Applicant:

Please re-submit your resume with address and phone number so we can add it to our database. Thank you for your interest in our company. We hope to speak with you soon.

Donna
Staffing Operations

From: scott47@yipee.com
Sent: Thursday, 20 August
To: Hotel (sales@blahblahblah.com)
Subject: great stay!

Dear Hotel People:

I'm writing to thank you for a wonderful reunion I recently had at your hotel. Sally and I had been high school sweethearts. She was so beautiful. She caught your eye like one of those pointy hook latches that used to dangle from screen doors and would fly up whenever you banged the door open again. About 6 months ago, I heard she was getting divorced, so I called to console her.

Fortunately, it was if we had never been apart! We talked about the old days, about our old suburban neighborhood, with picket fences that resembled Nancy Kerrigan's teeth. We decided to meet for weekend. I contacted one of your reservations clerk and he spoke with the wisdom that can only come from experience, like a guy who went blind because he looked at a solar eclipse without one of those boxes with a pinhole in it and now goes around the country speaking at high schools about the dangers of looking at a solar eclipse without the one of those boxes with a pinhole in it.

Finally, the weekend arrived. When she walked in, we raced across the lobby like two freight trains, one having left Cleveland at 6:36 p.m. traveling at 55 mph, the other from Topeka at 4:19 p.m. at a speed of 35 mph. Sirs, the whole weekend was fabulous! Frankly, it had a surreal quality, like when you're on vacation in another city and "Jeopardy" comes on at 7 p.m. instead of 7:30.

We are now planning to be married. I'm really hoping to have the event with you people. Otherwise, I will be as perplexed as a hacker who means to access T:flw.quid55328.com/aaakk/ch@ung but gets T:/flw.quidaaakk/ch@ung by mistake.

Sincerely, Scott Neumann

From: sales@blahblahblah.com
Sent: Thursday, 20 August
To: scott47@yipee.com
Subject: your reception

Scott:

Thank you for your e-mail dated August 20. My name is Julie and I am a
Catering Manger at the Hotel.
I would like to congratulate you on you on your recent engagement. We
would be happy to host your wedding reception at the Hotel. Please e-mail
back with your address and phone number so that I can get in contact with
you. Once I have received you prospective wedding date I can check for
space availability and give you prices. Here we have an excellent wedding
packages for receptions and ceremonies. Thank you again for your inquiry
and I look forward to speaking to you regarding your event.

Sincerely,

Julie Carden, Catering Sales Manager

From: scott47@yipee.com
Sent: Friday, 21 August
To: Sunny Sleep Center (info@blahblahblah.com)
Subject: important question

Dear Sleep Disorder People:

Why do they use the letter "Z" in cartoons to indicate sleeping?

To me, I would think they would use the letter "S" for Snoozing—SSSSSSSSSSSSSS. Or "N" for Night Night-NNNNNNNNNNNNN. Or even "EGSS" for "Everybody Get Some Shuteye".

I'm curious if you have an answer to this or what the feelings of a sleep expert would be regarding the letter "Z".

Sincerely,
Scott Neumann

In no way affiliated with the Neumann family of Northern Arizona

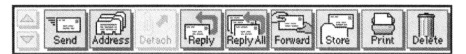

From: info@blahblahblah.com
Sent: Sunday, 23 August
To: scott47@yipee.com
Subject: question

Dear Scott,

One would think that with everything that is happening in our country as well as our WORLD, the last thing someone would be concerned about is the letter Z relating to sleep.!!!!! My explanation for this is that the letter Z most closely resembles the sound of snoring when a person is asleep. Hence,the ZZZZZZZZZ. Does that answer your question?

I hope so.

From: scott47@yipee.com
Sent: Tuesday, 21 July
To: Marathon Race (marathon@blahblahblah.com)
Subject: race info

Dear Marathon Race People:

I'm very interested in entering your 26.2 mile race. However, I can't run because I have very bad knees. But I am an excellent tumbler. As such, I'd like to roll the entire race.

Since the weather has improved, I've been able to roll almost 3 miles outside without stopping.

In my training, I've also gone out of my way to roll next to cars and runners on the street, and I've found that I'm very good at maintaining a straight line. I guess I was blessed with the straight line gene. My only problem appears to be figuring out a way to drink water. That, and broken beer bottles.

Can you send me a detailed map of your layout so I can familiarize myself with your course? I can tape it on my thigh so I'll know where I'm going. I think.

Sincerely,
Scott Neumann

From: marathon@blahblahblah.com
Sent: Tuesday, 21 July
To: scott47@yipee.com
Subject: race

Scott:

Please give me a call. I'm very interested in talking to you about our race.

Vince

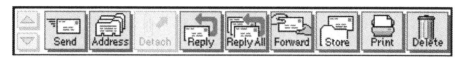

From: scott47@yipee.com
Sent: Saturday, 27 June
To: Karate School (afriedm@blahblahblah.net)
Subject: purchase request

Dear Martial Arts People:

I am interested in purchasing one of those white robes along with a black belt.

I do not wish to take lessons. I don't have the time nor the patience to learn anything new at this point in my life. I simply want to give the impression to friends and family that I have a attained a superior level of karate skill. I am sick and tired of being picked on at work and at family functions. And with a few choice "Hi—Yeeeee's!" thrown around, I believe people will finally begin to take me seriously. How much would you charge for the robe and black belt? And how soon could you ship them out to me? We have a family picnic next month. If I could have them by then, that would be a great place to unveil the new Bruce Lee Neumann.

I look forward to hearing back from you soon.

Sincerely, Scott Neumann

P.S. Do you sell karate club cards or something that I can carry in my wallet to indicate that I am at the pinnacle of karate success?

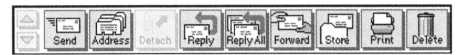

From: afriedm@blahblahblah.net
Sent: Sunday, 28 June
Sent: scott47@yipee.com
Subject: request

I must tell you that while uniforms and belts can be purchased, the skill, honor and certification of the belts can not. I would not sell you a belt. However, many martial arts stores will, and some unscrupulous instructors will even sell you the certification. The question you must ask yourself is what will be gained by doing this? Rethink your course of action. It is a hazardous one at best.

Sincerely,
Sa Bum Albert

From: scott47@yipee.com
Sent: Sunday, 14 June
To: Dept. of Corrections (vj@blahblahblah.gov)
Subject: prison performance

Dear Correctional Facility People:

It is my great pleasure to offer your Prison a free performance of our award-winning rendition of "Le Folies Bergere".

Sirs, you will find that our show truly is a spectacular rendition of this classic story. And I believe we have enhanced the age-old stage drama even more with an incredible array of sequined costumes and diamond-studded nipple rings. For our all-male troupe, we've also added some special numbers to the show including: "Crazy About Heinies" and "Love To Love You Again And Again And Again."

We believe that this is the type of quality entertainment that the incarcerated men in this country are looking for. You should know that when we performed in Ohio, we had 4 inmates join our show on stage. They did a great job—and their tanned, toned, prison-built bodies blended in perfectly. It was delicious.

We hope to hear back from you as soon as possible so we can make the proper arrangements.

Sincerely, Scott Neumann

Artistic Director, American International

"Internationally Know For American Dance"

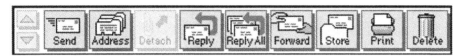

From: vj@blahblahblah.gov
Sent: Friday, 19 June
To: scott47@yipee.com
Subject: performance

Sir:

Your offer to provide a free stage performance for inmates in the North Carolina Department of Correction is appreciated, but respectfully declined.

Keith, Chief of Program Services

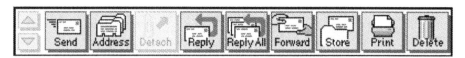

From: scott47@yipee.com
Sent: Monday, 1 June
To: Trident Gum (Con@blahblahblah.com)
Subject: name usage

Dear Trident Chewing Gum People:

My uncle, Jimmy Dent, is running for our local city council. A seat has been vacated due to the sudden disappearance of Clarence "Big Momma" Hopkins. My uncle has asked me to help him run his campaign and I believe I've come up with a catchy slogan. There are now bumper stickers, billboards and t-shirts all over town with the phrase: "Try Dent".

Last week, someone casually mentioned that this might be some sort of conflict with the name of your gum. I don't see how this is possible, but I'm writing to you just to be safe. I hope it's ok, because we've invested a whole lot of money into this stuff and my uncle would be really pissed at me if it wasn't.

Please let me know ASAP. If there's a problem, I may have to resort to our other slogan: "There Is Too Such A Thing As A Good Dent!" Thank you for your time.

Sincerely,

Scott Neumann

Campaign Manager and Long Distance Blinker

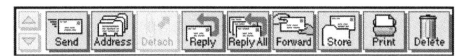

From: con@blahblahblah.com
Sent: Wednesday, 3 June
To: scott47@yipee.com
Subject: usage

Sir:

Thank you for visiting our website. Regarding your question, you would need to contact our Legal Department.

Chip
Consumer Affairs

From: scott47@yipee.com
Sent: Friday, 29 May
To: City of Aspen (Dave@blahblahblah.com)
Subject: concerned!

Dear City Official People:

I've recently read that the city of Aspen is changing its name to Padoopysville. This makes no sense to me.

Changing Aspen to Padoopysville would be a big, big mistake. Bigger than the time I almost married that girl. Is there anyone I can write to express my concern over this issue? I've found that letter writing can really make a difference in cases like these. I recently got a local sanitation law changed that forced us to separate orange rinds from the rest of our garbage.

I hope to hear back from you.

Sincerely,

Scott Neumann

From: Dave@blahblahblah.com
Sent: Monday, 1 June
To:scott47@yipee.com
Subject: response

Sir:

I believe someone is playing some sort of sick joke with you. I have not heard anything like that and I really doubt that there is any sort of truth to that.

Thanks,

Dave

From: scott47@yipee.com
Sent: Monday, 1 June
To: Best Used Car (bestsales@blahblahblah.com)
Subject: search

Dear Used Automobile Dealership People:

I have a used car in mind that I'm hoping you can help me find. The car I'm looking for is blue with black tires. I don't really care about the manufacturer, what year it is, what kind of engine it has, or the mileage. I just want a blue car with black tires. And I don't mean a metallic blue, either. I'm looking for a sky blue. I know I may sound picky, but that's the kind of person I am: I know what I want and I go for it. Do you have a car like this? And do you offer a warranty that guarantees that blue is the original color of the vehicle?

If you have this car, please respond to me ASAP. I will be there as soon as I can. It may take me a few days, since I will be using a combination of public transportation, a pogo stick and a unicycle to get there.

Thank you for your time.

Sincerely,
Scott Neumann,
Rap Music Recording Artist

From: bestsales@blahblahblah.com
Sent: Monday, 1 June
To: scott47@yipee.com
Subject: car

SCOTT, WE HAVE THE UNIT, IT WILL EVEN HOLD YOUR UNI-CYCLE...IT IS 1966 FOR MUSTANG IT IS THE CAR FOR YOU...I JUST KNOW IT...COME ON DOWN

SCOTT...KELLY

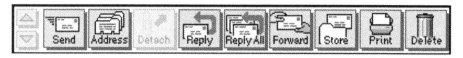

From: scott47@yipee.com
Sent: Tuesday, 19 May
To: Worldwide Business Etiquette (ice@blahblahblah.net)
Subject: question

Dear Business Etiquette People:

I was recently attending a meeting with one of our international clients in Kazakhstan. He's a pretty big guy, and as I found out later, he wrestled professionally under the pseudonym, "Scary Harry, the Maniac from Northern Wisconsin."

At any rate, in the middle of our discussions over a new contract, the conversation got quite heated, and the next thing I knew, he had me on the floor in a figure-four leg lock. Then with his people cheering him on, he jumped off the table onto my chest, he lifted me, slammed my head into the chair, and held me upside down and dropped me on my head. The only way I could get him off me was to reach underneath and twist his testicles. He immediately jumped up and said that wasn't fair.

Although he later signed the contract, I still find myself a bit uncomfortable regarding this situation. Is this some sort of business ritual in Kazakhstan, or was he just trying to bully me? I have to go back and see him again next month and I'm wondering if I should bring some tights with me.

Any help would be greatly appreciated.

Sincerely,

Scott Neumann

I've heard that in Budapest they tickle foreigners. Is that true?

From: ice@blahblahblah.net
Sent: Tuesday, 19 May
To: scott47@yipee.com
Subject: response

Dear Scott:

There is no such a custom in Kazakhstan to wrestle with business partners. It is hard to give any advice as to what you should do without knowing the actual circumstances.

Sincerely,
Worldwide Business

From: scott47@yipee.com
Sent: Friday, 8 May
To: Chicago Cubs (comments@blahblahblah.com)
Subject: wedding?????

Dear Baseball Team People:

You seem like a fun organization. That's why I'd like to get married and have a traditional wedding at one of your games. It would be a dream come true for us. Bruce and I are both huge baseball fans.

I've contacted some other teams and they seem a bit leery. I guess because they don't want a chuppah on their field. We're very flexible about dates. And other things, if you know what I mean.

I think baseball is the greatest game on earth. I just love the smell of the fresh leather. I hope to hear back from you soon.

Sincerely,

Scott "No Longer Looking For A" Neu-mann

P.S. I would like to have the wedding at first base too, since that's as far as I let him go on our first date!

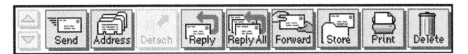

From: comments@blahblahblah.com
Sent: Friday, 8 May
To: scott47@yipee.com
Subject: thank you

Sir:

Thank you for contacting the Chicago Cubs.

While we may not be able to respond to all e-mail correspondence personally, we appreciate your writing and will pass your idea onto the appropriate people.

From: scott47@yipee.com
Sent: Monday, 1 June
To: Dream Analyst (Dlover@blahblahblah.com)
Subject: my dream

Dear "Tell Me What My Dream Meant" People:

Last Thursday night I dreamt I was performing a conclave vector analysis on a lateral axis. Later in the dream, I positioned the microprocessor three degrees from the valence area, and then calculated the average weight of the sub-woofer. Then I re-tracked the convex semi-transistor and used a process control model and a drive system sequential application to complete the program.

I believe this dream may be sending me some sort of message about my relationship with my mother and my obsession with raisins. Any help would be appreciated.

Thank you for your time. And God bless.

Sincerely,
Pastor Scott Neumann

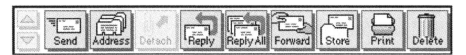

From: Dlover@blahblahblah.com
Sent: Tuesday, 2 June
To: scott47@yipee.com
Subject: your dream

Dear Pastor Neumann:

On my web site I promised every dreamer that I would answer their-mail…so I shall. Thank your for visiting our web site, I hope that you looked around, and I am sorry that it has taken me this long to answer you; it usually takes less than a few days. The last time that I told a person that wrote to me that their dream was less then genuine and that I had a hard time believing that they actually dreamt it…they got very insulted …but it's OK because they were playing around with me and then had an attack of guilt. I will not tell you that you are lying about this dream, but I will say that if you want me to give you an impression of what it means…that you please write it in a form of the English language that I will be able to understand, because currently—to me—it sounds like non-sense. I cannot follow what you are saying, and I don't know how it could possibly be related to your mother.

Peace and happy dreaming,
Silvia

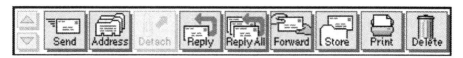

From: scott47@yipee.com
Sent: Wednesday, 27 May
To: Eastern Research (rob@blahblahblah.edu)
Subject: Chinese Exclusion Act Concerns

Dear Scholarly Sir:

I was recently reading up on the Chinese Exclusion Act of 1882 that limited the entrance of those of Chinese persuasion to this country. Yesterday someone told me that the Act is going to be updated to now also limit the intake of egg rolls in the Eastern United States, followed by won ton soup in 2006. Admittedly, I'm no political expert, but when more people find out about this, there's going to be some sort of uproar, isn't there? Chinese food is very popular these days.

Who can I contact regarding this situation? I'm a concerned citizen and I want to do my part to help. I recently initiated a letter writing campaign to save an old piece of chalk at my son's grade school.

I hope to hear back from you soon.

Sincerely,

Scott Neumann

p.s. What's next? Chinese Checkers?

From: rob@blahblahblah.edu
Sent: Sunday, 31 May
To: scott47@yipee.com
Subject: Chinese Exclusion Act Concerns

Scott,

I commend your willingness to get involved—you are clearly a model citizen. To ease your worries, though, you will probably be surprised to learn that egg rolls are not a particularly "Chinese" dish. I have been living in China for the better part of the last two years and have had spring rolls only twice, once at a Japanese restaurant. it seems that egg rolls, like fortune cookies, are more a manifestation of American Chinese food, rather than the authentic thing here in the land of 1.2 billion. thus, despite the upcoming egg roll embargo, I'm sure native US Chinese restaurants will be able to fill all the existing demand for egg rolls in the US.

Cheers,
Rob

From: scott47@yipee.com
Sent: Wednesday, 27 May
To: Shipping Company (David@blahblahblah.com)
Subject: delivery

Dear Delivery Service People:

My brother collects animal droppings, and I have some that I'd like to send to him. If I send this by mail, I run the risk of the entire collection flattening out during the delivery process, which obviously renders it worthless.

Do you provide some type of insurance guarantee that these droppings will remain intact, in their semi-round shape? These droppings come from a rare hybrid of a rabbit and duck from our local zoo. It's called a duckbit.

Any assistance you can provide me would be greatly appreciated. And if you could do so fairly quickly, that would be even better. They're starting to smell.

Sincerely,
Scott Neumann, Tracing Enthusiast

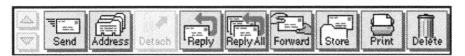

From: David@blahblahblah.com
Sent: Saturday, 30 May
To: scott47@yipee.com
Subject: delivery

Sir:

We're sorry, however, animal droppings can neither be shipped by us noninsured against loss of roundness.

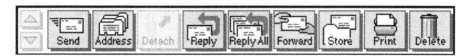

From: scott47@yipee.com
Sent: Wednesday, 27 May
To: Estate Law Firm (fuller@blahblahblah.com)
Subject: possible lawsuit???

Dear Legal Professional People Sirs:

Recently, I happened to come across some paperwork that seems to indicate that my great, great, great grandfather invented the salad fork. I'm not a legal expert, but these papers do appear to show that he had some sort of patent on the idea of a "fork with reduced prong length."

If this is in fact valid—and it seems to be—can we sue salad fork manufacturers for all those years of use without our consent? Or what about lettuce growers? Couldn't you make a good legal argument that if it wasn't for the salad fork, people would have to eat their salads using large regular forks, so they'd eat more at a time, which means salad dressing makers would be forced to make more and incur additional production costs?

I'm not greedy or anything. I just want to get what I deserve as an heir to the Salad Fork throne.
I hope to hear back from you soon.

Sincerely, Scott Neumann

P.S. The funny thing is, I hate salad. Just hate it.

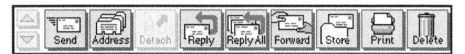

From: fuller@blahblahblah.com
Sent: Wednesday, 27 May
To: scott47@yipee.com
Subject: legal question

Mr. Neumann:

It depends on whether or not he actually was granted a patent. Patent's do expire after 17 years (there are some limited extensions.) I would be glad to look at the papers and tell you what you may have. The paper itself may have antique value. You are welcome to send me an email with an attachment if possible or mail me a copy. You will not be charged for me just to see what you have.

From: scott47@yipee.com
Sent: Saturday, 4 April
To: Science Conference (siv@blahblahblah.com)
Subject: impt. question

Dear Important Gathering of Smart People People:

Greetings! I've been in your website and have been reading about your upcoming conference on Melioidosis. I'm particularly interested in this fatal bacterial disease caused by an environmental saprophyte.

Sirs, I'm contemplating on attending your meeting, but before I decide, could you tell me what time you people eat lunch? I realize you're foreign and all, but my body is very funny about being off schedule and I need to know this before I determine whether or not to attend. I need to eat between 12:15 and 12:19 everyday. And I'm assuming you will have American food because that is what most people like. Could you possibly let me know what the meal plans are, and what time you all plan on letting us eat? As soon as possible, if that's possible.

I sincerely hope I can make it to your conference. I'm real excited about getting a snowglobe from your city to add to my collection.

Sincerely, Scott Neumann

P.S. I know a girl named Melio.

From: siv@blahblahblah.com
Sent: Saturday, 4 April
To: scott47@yipee.com
Subject: question

Dear Scott:

The lunch time is noon to 1 PM.

Visanu

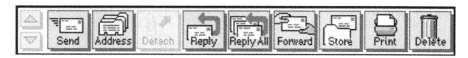

From: scott47@yipee.com
Sent: Monday, 27 April
To: Ef@blahblahblah.com
Subject: M & M's

Dear Candy Coated Candy People:

I have to tell you how much I love M & M's. The problem though is that I'm colorblind. I can't tell a green M & M from a red one from an orange one. And as much as I love M & M's, I feel I'm missing part of the "M & M experience" because they're all the same to me.

Question: how difficult would it be to manufacture a line of textured M& M's? Here's my thought:

Light Brown: Bumpy
Green: Grainy (like smashed glass)
Yellow: Jello-y
Red: Wavy
Dark Brown: Warm to the Touch
Blue: Vibrating

I'm telling you, I have some colorblind friends and these would really go over big with them, too. Would this complicate your manufacturing process in any way? I have no idea.

I look forward to hearing back from you.

Sincerely, Scott Neumann

P.S. Have you ever considered M & M's on a stick?

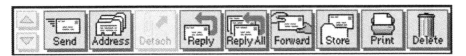

From: Ef@blahblahblah.com
Sent: Monday, 27 April
To: scott47@yipee.com
Subject: M & M's

Hi Scott, Thank you for your feedback. You have some great ideas. We will pass them on.

Greetings,

Your friends at M&M's

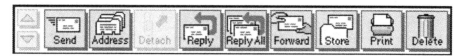

From: scott47@yipee.com
Sent: Friday, 18 September
To: Ad Agency (info@blahblahblah.com)
Subject: ad question

Dear Advertising Agency People:

I love commercials. Do you do the funny one where the dog talks like a little Mexican guy? That is one funny commercial. I think it was funnier than the show I was watching before I was watching the dog that talks like a little Mexican guy. It was a show with a guy in a blue shirt talking about something to a woman with black hair who kind of looked like Pamela Anderson if Pamela Anderson had black hair and weighed about 100 pounds more and was shorter. I love Pamela Anderson.

If you didn't do the dog commercial, can you tell me who did? I would like to thank them for giving me gas from laughing so hard.

I had an idea once about a dog that walked around all day and ate garbage from the streets, but I never did anything with it. Looking back on it, I think the dog that talks like a little Mexican guy is funnier.

Sincerely,

Scott Neumann

"The Man of 1,000 Voices"

From: info@blahblahblah.com
Sent: Friday, 18 September
To: scott47@yipee.com
Subject: answer

Scott:

Nope, we didn't do the commercial. It is funny, isn't it? Sorry though, don't know who did it.

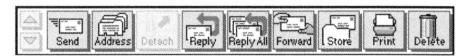

From: scott47@yipee.com
Sent: Friday, 25 September
To: Scott Neumann (cneum@blahblahblah.edu)
Subject: name

Dear Scott Neumann:

Sir, after typing MY name, Scott Neumann, into an e-mail database search, I was shocked to discover that you have been going by the name Scott Neumann as well. Can't you people leave me alone?

Sir, I have contacted my attorney and he is in the process of issuing a cease and desist order to prevent you from the use of my name, Scott Neumann. Sir, the fact is, I've had this name since birth; it is on my birth certificate; hence, it is mine. Furthermore, I have a very important job in a very important company and I travel the country a great deal for very important meetings with very important clients. I cannot afford any type of confusion with another "Scott Neumann."

Sir, if you will discontinue use of my name, I will instruct my attorney to halt the background check he is currently running to damage your credibility should I choose to take this case to court and seek punitive damages.

Sir, I expect to hear back from you soon. Whoever you are.

Sincerely,

Scott Neumann. THE Scott Neumann

From: cneum@blahblahblah.edu
Sent: Friday, 25 September
To: scott47@yipee.com
Subject: name

Dear Scott,

I am sorry to hear that you are so distraught over this issue. The fact of the matter is, the name Scott Neumann has been in my family for many decades. My great, great uncle twice removed (maternal side) was named Scott Neumann (his name has an umlaut which I cannot type) and was a sheepherder in eastern Germany. Upon immigrating to the states, he changed his name to Scott(correct spelling now), but kept the original spelling of Neumann. Hence, I believe property rights of "Scott Neumann" belong to my family. Since I am the only Scott Neumann in my family at this time I hold all the rights and privileges that go with this name. Therefore, I ask that you give me your important job in this important company and allow me to importantly meet with your important clients. You may still travel the country at your leisure as I am a quadriplegic and cannot easily maneuver my wheel chair down a jet way. In light of the aggressive attitude I sensed in your letter, I have filed a counter-suit against you and your entire family. And your lawyer. In the meantime, can you please tell me where your desk is so that I may importantly go there on Monday and begin my new job.

Sincerely yours,
Scott Neumann

www.ingramcontent.com/pod-product-compliance
Lightning Source LLC
Chambersburg PA
CBHW051243050326
40689CB00007B/1051